The Kingdom of Kush

A Captivating Guide to an Ancient African Kingdom in Nubia That Once Ruled Egypt

Free Bonus from Captivating History (Available for a Limited time)

Hi History Lovers!

Now you have a chance to join our exclusive history list so you can get your first history ebook for free as well as discounts and a potential to get more history books for free! Simply visit the link below to join.

Captivatinghistory.com/ebook

Also, make sure to follow us on Facebook, Twitter and Youtube by searching for Captivating History.

Contents

FREE BONUS FROM CAPTIVATING HISTORY (AVAILABLE FOR A LIMITED TIME) 1

INTRODUCTION 3

CHAPTER 1 – NUBIA AND THE EMERGENCE OF THE KINGDOM OF KUSH 5

CHAPTER 2 – FROM ALARA TO THE TWENTY-FIFTH DYNASTY 19

CHAPTER 3 – THE RULERS OF THE TWENTY-FIFTH DYNASTY 29

CHAPTER 4 – RELATIONS BETWEEN KUSH AND EGYPT CONTINUE 42

CHAPTER 5 – KUSH BETWEEN THE 6TH AND 3RD CENTURIES 50

CHAPTER 6 – THE MEROITIC DYNASTY 60

CHAPTER 7 – THE LAST CENTURIES OF THE KINGDOM OF KUSH.... 73

CHAPTER 8 – THE SOCIETY OF KUSH.. 81

CONCLUSION.. 92

REFERENCES 95

Introduction

The Kingdom of Kush was completely forgotten once it met its end. The stories of its might didn't survive in the cultures of its successor kingdoms, possibly because Christianization soon followed, which required the people of the Nubian region to turn toward the east and the myths of the Christian messiah. There was no more room for the divine rulers, Amun and Re, or a place for their sons, the kings of Kush. The kingdom continued to exist in the stories of some classical writers, but it was often considered as nothing more than a distant, probably even imaginary, kingdom, where the uncivilized savages lived.

With the renewed interest in the classical arts of Greece and Rome, the Renaissance rediscovered the existence of Kush. Still, it was not explored until Napoleon's expedition to Egypt in 1798. Even then, it was seen as a part of Egyptian culture. The discoveries made by the 18th- and 19th-century explorers proved there were, in fact, two separate cultures. However, this explanation was greatly influenced by Darwinism. Scholars presented the entirety of Africa as a place where civilized white men ruled over the "uncivilized negroes." Kush was no exception to them, and the general opinion was that Egypt ruled over the uncivilized Kushites. Even the rule of the Twenty-Fifth Dynasty was observed as nothing more than the less fortunate Kushites imitating the superior Egyptians.

It was not until the early 20th century that the Kingdom of Kush received its rightful place in history. When the first archaeological survey of Nubia took place between 1907 and 1911, the distinctive cultural aspects of the Kingdom of Kush emerged, and it was finally seen as a separate entity from Egypt. The detailed chronology for the Kingdom of Kush was suggested, and archaeologists from all over the world came to explore the uniqueness of the Middle Nile Region. However, early modern archaeologists were greatly influenced by the Renaissance opinion that the "Hamitic" civilization ruled over the uncivilized African world, and this opinion was hard to change. Unfortunately, the lack of funding and interest led to the neglect of the excavation sites in Nubia.

The extension of the Aswan Dam in the 1960s threatened to submerge a large portion of the Nubian excavation sites under the water forever. To prevent this from happening, UNESCO organized an archaeological expedition, whose purpose was to preserve everything found between the First and Second Cataracts of the Nile. During the UNESCO salvation period, over 1,000 new excavation sites were found, and an enormous amount of archaeological work was completed. This resulted in a change of opinion about the culture of the Middle Nile Region. No longer were scholars indoctrinated by the Renaissance view of the Kushites as "uncivilized negroes" ruled by superior Egyptians. Finally, pragmatism won, and the real truth about the Kingdom of Kush and its rulers saw the light of day. From the 1960s onward, the understanding and recognition of the Kingdom of Kush began. The history of Kush could finally be written.

Chapter 1 – Nubia and the Emergence of the Kingdom of Kush

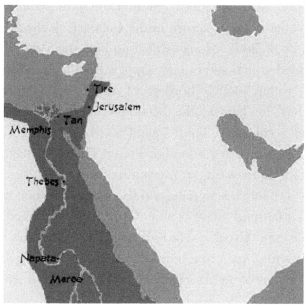

Kush in 700 BCE, at its maximum extent
https://en.wikipedia.org/wiki/Kingdom_of_Kush#/media/
File:Kushite_empire_700bc.jpg

Nubia, a region perhaps more mysterious than Egypt, tickles the imagination of people around the world because it was misunderstood. Although it belonged to Egypt at some points in history, it was never really an integral part of the ancient kingdom. In fact, it was the birthplace of various civilizations, and modern findings even suggest it was the birthplace of the first pharaohs and Egypt itself. One of the most known kingdoms of Nubia is none other than the Kingdom of Kush. To follow the origin of the Kingdom of Kush, we have to see what lies deep beneath the Nubian sands, what was there before Egypt started spreading its influence on the region (or was it vice versa?)

The region of Nubia lay south of Egypt, alongside the flow of the River Nile. It occupied the whole Nile River Valley south of the Egyptian city of Aswan to the capital of Sudan: Khartoum. It was at Aswan that the first shallow waters of the great river flowed, and it was known as the First Cataract of the Nile. The First Cataract doesn't exist anymore, as the modern Aswan Dam now stands there. The region of Nubia was also known as the Cataracts of the Nile, as there used to be six shallows through which no boat was able to sail. Nubia itself was divided into three parts: upper, middle, and lower. Lower Nubia was within today's borders of Egypt, and it occupied the territory from the First to the Second Cataract. Middle Nubia lay between the Second and Third Cataracts, while Upper Nubia spread over all the territories to the south from the Third Cataract.

The name Nubia wasn't in use during the Old or New Kingdoms of Egypt. It is of much later date, and it came about when the Meroitic Kingdom fell (around the 4th century CE). Egyptians called this region Kush, while the Greeks referred to it as Aethiopia (Ethiopia). However, it is important to remember that the Greeks used this name for several regions of the African continent, as its meaning, "The Land of the Burnt-Face," not so subtly suggested that the area was occupied by a dark-skinned population. The name Nubia came from the nomadic Noba people who lived there after the Meroitic kingdom, around the 4th century BCE.

When prehistoric Egypt emerged as a political power in around 3500 BCE (give or take a few centuries, as scholars cannot agree on the exact date), a civilization already existed in the Nubian territory. They are labeled as the A-group culture, and they had already developed trade with what was then Egypt. Around 3100 BCE, Egypt's First Dynasty started a new era by uniting the kingdoms of Lower and Upper Egypt. It seems that, at this point, Nubia was a part of the newly unified kingdom, and some scholars even suggest the A-group culture influenced the unification of the Nile Valley.

The people who settled in Nubia during prehistoric Egypt were a mixture of ancient tribes of Sudan, the sub-Saharan regions, and even the regions to the west. This mixture produced a unique culture, which would give birth to what is known as the Egyptian and Nubian culture. However, the A-group peoples disappeared from the region around the 28th century BCE. It is speculated that they were completely absorbed into the Egyptian lifestyle, for it seems that up until 2500 BCE, Nubia was deserted. Another possibility is that it was occupied by a much inferior culture, named the B-group, who left no trails in history. However, in the 24th century BCE, the emergence of the C-group started, and archaeological findings prove that they were related to the A-group. It is believed the C-group were the descendants of the A-group finally returning back to the region, although it is also possible the A-group never even left. But the culture of the Nubian region went through a renaissance period and returned to its roots. They are known as the Kerma culture to scholars, as the center of their civilization was in the kingdom's capital city of Kerma.

During the Middle Kingdom of Egypt (2040–1640 BCE), the relations with the Nubian Kerma civilization were mixed. There were certainly some armed conflicts, as Egypt annexed some of the Nubian territories, but there were also times of peaceful trade and cooperation. There is even evidence of intermarriages and friendship between the two cultures. Egypt was always interested in the territories of Lower Nubia because it was a gateway to the trade with Upper Nubia and the exotic parts of Africa. The pharaohs of the Middle

Kingdom tried to gain control of the region both through war and through diplomacy.

At first, the Kerma kingdom was thought to be just one of the small states that occupied the Nile Valley at the time of the Middle Kingdom. However, later findings proved that Kerma spread its influence on much larger territories. The city of Kerma, in today's Sudan, was thought to be the only archaeological site of the Kerma culture. As the explorations continued to the south, toward what was once Egypt's border with the Nubian regions, scholars were surprised to discover more Kerma settlements and graveyards.

The size of the Kerma territory proves that this civilization was an influential political power in the region. No wonder they were of interest to Egypt. They were both potential allies or possible enemies, and they were capable of rivaling the pharaoh's power. The Kerma kingdom even inspired the Egyptians to raise a series of fortifications along their southern border, for example, such as those at Buhen and Qubban in the Middle Nile Region. Whether these were used for defense or for an attack remains unknown.

It is interesting that these Egyptian fortresses were also used as trade and culture centers where both Egyptian and Nubian populations were involved in businesses. This was probably due to the fact that gold routes from the mines of the southern Nubian regions lay here, at the border of the two kingdoms. Egypt needed the gold to continue flowing its way, and one of the best ways to secure it was through peace. Some historians even suggest that the absorption of Lower Nubia by Egypt was gradual and that the Kerma rulers were compliant. Others suggest that it was the rising power of the rich middle class of Kerma that forced Egypt's hand to send military expeditions to the region.

The connection between Egypt and Nubia was constant, and the influence the two cultures had on each other is evident. Both Egyptian and Nubian Kerma rulers used very similar symbols to define their position. But it was during the New Kingdom that the two cultures became almost indistinguishable. While the texts of the early New

Kingdom referred to the Nubian regions as Ta-Seti, the "Curved Land" or the "Land of the Bow" (as people there were famous for their archery skills), it was during Kerma's declining years that the first mention of Kush occurred. The Kerma people probably spoke the Kushite language, and it is believed that they were the first founders of the Kingdom of Kush, or rather that the Kushites rose out of the Kerma civilization. It was these Kushites who fought Egypt's attempt of annexation during the rule of Pharaoh Kamose (around 1500 BCE) and his successor Ahmose I (1552-1527 BCE). The texts the two pharaohs left behind are the first written source in which the Kerma kingdom is referred to as Kush instead of Ta-Seti.

It is not known how the Kingdom of Kush got its name in the first place. To Egyptians, it was always known as Ta-Seti, even before the Old Kingdom. But it is unknown what the native name of Nubia was in prehistoric times. Maybe it was always Kush or some version of this name, and Egypt started using its native name when it recognized the importance of the region. The northernmost region of Nubia, which bordered Egypt, was known as Wawat, or "Lower Nubia," while the alternative name for the region was Ta-Neshy, the "Land of the Black People." This is similar to the Greek Aethiopia, the "Land of the Burnt-Face." So, both Egyptians and Greeks recognized the indigenous people of Nubia, but it is uncertain if these names referred to all of Nubia or only certain parts.

Egypt's annexation of the territories of Lower Nubia was successful, and it continued to grab lands farther to the south under Pharaoh Amenhotep I (1525-1504 BCE, disputed) and Thutmose (Tuthmosis) I (1506-1494 BCE). They conquered Sai and Bugdumbush, the two major Kerma civilization centers besides the city of Kerma. Finally, Egypt reached the gold mining areas of the eastern desert, where the Korosko road met the Nile. The Korosko road was an ancient land route that was used by the trade caravans to bypass the unassailable waters of the Second, Third, and Fourth Cataracts of the Nile. During the rule of Thutmose III (1479-1425 BCE), the full control of Nubia was established, and Egypt extended

9

all the way to the Fourth Cataract of the Nile. This, too, was a gold-producing territory, and as such, it was very important to Egypt. There, at the small mountain of Gebel Barkal, Thutmose III founded the southernmost Egyptian city of Napata in around 1460 BCE.

The Nubian region under Egypt was overseen by a viceroy known as the "King's Sons." This was just a title, as they were not actually related to the pharaoh, though they might have been members of the royal family. During the reign of Amenhotep II (1427–1401/1397 BCE), the title was changed to "King's Sons of Kush." The viceroys were always chosen from the ranks of royal bureaucrats, chariotry, or stable administrators. They were responsible for the people of Nubia, and their main task was to collect taxes and tributes. The gold mines were also under their watchful eyes, as they were directly responsible for the production of gold. The viceroys had full command over the Nubian military troops, but it seems there was a "battalion-commander of Kush" as well. This means the viceroy probably only had the power to command the army if he invoked his right. Otherwise, the command was in the hands of the battalion-commander. Wawat (Lower Nubia) and Kush (Upper Nubia) had their own deputy governors, who were appointed by the viceroy.

Nubia spent centuries under Egyptian rule, and it is no wonder the cultural influence between the two regions was so deep. From the first occupation in the Middle Kingdom until the end of the New Kingdom, the Kushite territories underwent extensive building projects. Temples and monuments were erected to celebrate the Egyptian gods and pharaohs. Even whole cities were founded by the temple-cults, and gradually, they became economic centers. In Wawat, two major cities sprouted as the residency for the deputy governors: Faras and Aniba. Similar cities in Kush were Soleb and Amara. They were also military settlements, and they quickly prospered and became the powerhouses of the region's economy.

The Nubian towns were surrounded by fertile lands, which the native population extensively cultivated. But the land was not a possession of the people. It was owned by the temples, pharaohs, members of the royal family, high-office holders, and probably the wealthy locals, who were descendants of the indigenous princes. The commoners only had the right to work the land, probably for a percentage of the harvest.

Egyptian cults were responsible for wielding much influence over the Nubian lands of Wawat and Kush. The temples, which were dedicated to gods such as Horus, Amun-Re, and Ptah, were built all over the country. These cults were closely tied with the worship of the pharaoh, who was seen as a divinity on earth. Nubia also accepted the cults of Hathor and Isis, although in a slightly changed and localized form. Pharaohs such as Thutmose III and Amenhotep III erected temples in which they were worshiped as living rulers. This wasn't an uncommon practice, but it was new to Nubia. The peak of pharaoh worship occurred during the rule of Ramesses II (1279–1212 BCE), who introduced the monumental rock-cut temples in Nubia. Before this, rock was hauled from different places. During Ramesses's rule, the temples were directly cut into the face of a small mountain or rock formation.

The level of Egyptianization the Nubian society went through greatly depended on the social status of the individuals. The elite families were educated in Egyptian schools, and after a few decades, they even started adopting Egyptian names. When they died, they were buried according to the Egyptian tradition. It is, in fact, the mortuary customs that inform us the most about the level of Egyptianization the locals went through. Due to the material evidence found around the dig sites, it was, at first, wrongly assumed the Nubian society as a whole was integrated into Egyptian norms equally. However, the material evidence only shows that the Egyptian economy was strong; thus, it would have been normal for the locals to start using the items of the superior culture. So, it is safer to rely on the burial customs, and they reveal quite a bit. The common people of Nubia, both in the cities and in the countryside, lack the Egyptian religious aspects in their mortuary customs. They did use Egyptian burial equipment, but they also integrated their own customs and mortuary rights. This is plainly evident through the lack of inscriptions of the names of the deceased, as well as through the survival of the indigenous religion in the form of iconography.

It seems the indigenous people of Nubia buried their dead, dedicating them to the local goddess *Nhsmks*. She is never mentioned in the Egyptian religion, at least according to evidence archaeologists have found so far. This is the main problem with ancient religions, for much evidence still lies buried deep beneath the ground. For now, the main belief is that the Nubian indigenous culture survived alongside the newly introduced Egyptian one, at least among the commoners.

The End of Egyptian Dominion

Egypt dominated Nubia for nearly five centuries (1550-1069 BCE), and it successfully integrated the whole region under its administration. The extension of the Egyptian kingdom's territories was regarded as its royal duty, and every pharaoh had to engage the neighboring kingdoms in a territorial war. It is possible that was how Nubia came under Egypt's dominion. But the extension stopped at the Fourth Cataract of the Nile, and it seems as if the Egyptians lost interest in further conquest. While there is strong evidence to suggest the propaganda against the local kings in the far south, Egypt never took those territories under its full control. This might be because the royal duties of "conquering new territories" and "repulsing the enemies of the state" had not been regarded as sacred since the rule of Ramesses III (1186-1154 BCE).

Even though Nubia was well assimilated into the Egyptian culture, especially the elite descendants of the indigenous rulers, the territory experienced a good deal of rebellions. There are records of numerous uprisings occurring between 1401 and 1186. There is no evidence that suggests the cause for these rebellions, but there were military conflicts in Nubian territory under almost every ruler until the Twentieth Dynasty. Modern scholars suggest the reason for some of the conflicts might be that the Nubians were reluctant to lose their control over the gold-producing areas.

At the end of the Twentieth Dynasty, Egypt withdrew from Upper Nubia, leaving the control of Napata and other economic centers of the south in the hands of indigenous rulers. Even though the Egyptian presence diminished, that doesn't mean Upper Nubia gained its independence. It seems that local rulers of Nubia were not treated as Egypt's vassals, unlike the Libyan and Puntite princes. Some believe that Egypt's withdrawal wasn't a sudden decision of a pharaoh but rather a gradual process. According to this theory, it was Ramesses III who retreated toward the north, creating a new southern border at Kawa. After Ramesses IV (1144–1136 BCE), Egypt withdrew even farther north.

However, there is evidence that the regions were still under viceroyalty power even during the reign of Ramesses IX (1125–1107). In his tomb, there is a depiction of Nubians bringing tribute and even granting agricultural land to the pharaoh. This means that, even though the Egyptian grasp over Nubia was still in place, it was very weak and about to collapse. During the reign of Ramesses IX, the Egyptian territories in Nubia extended only up until the Second Cataract, where the ruins of the Egyptian settlement of Buhen can still be found.

But it remains unknown if Egypt retreated peacefully or due to the aggression of the indigenous people. Even more confusion is raised due to the fact Egypt withdrew from Palestine at the same time. This leads one to the conclusion that the political and economic power of the late Twentieth Dynasty was declining. With it, the weakening of the central government came, and it was only a matter of time before the surviving indigenous socio-political structure returned to Nubia.

There is very strong written evidence of a civil war occurring in the region around the city of Thebes. The conflict erupted between Pinehesy, Viceroy of Kush, and Amenhotep, the High Priest of Amun of Thebes. The reason for the conflict is unknown, but it seems that the high priest was agitated by Pinehesy's quick rise to power. Pinehesy was given control over the military and the royal granaries, which were symbols of political and economic power. Until that point, they had been in the hands of Amenhotep. The conflict greatly escalated when Pinehesy's troops started looting the temples of Thebes, which they were supposed to protect. The viceroy enjoyed the control he had over the Nubian region, and his actions created the sense as if Upper and Middle Egypt were occupied.

Amenhotep complained to Pharaoh Ramesses XI and gained his protection against Pinehesy. The king ordered the viceroy to move his troops out of Thebes, but Pinehesy revolted and started a rebellion, which caused the whole region to suffer war, famine, and various atrocities committed by the military troops. In the nineteenth year of Ramesses XI's reign, Pinehesy was forced to retreat to Lower Nubia, where he started ruling as an independent king in around 1071 BCE.

El-Kurru and the Unification of the Successor Kingdoms

A 4ᵗʰ century BCE pyramid in El-Kurru
https://en.wikipedia.org/wiki/El-Kurru#/media/File:Al-Kurru,main_pyramid.jpg

The development of events between the 11ᵗʰ and 8ᵗʰ centuries BCE remains obscure, but they are still important to understand how the Kingdom of Kush emerged. Egypt's withdrawal from the southern Nubian territories may have been connected with the story of the rebellious Viceroy Pinehesy, who became the ruler of the territories beyond the Second Cataract. Even though Egypt returned and asserted control over the gold mines in the area after his death, it never managed to completely annex Nubia again.

The reemergence of the native political system was possible because Egypt never fully implemented a colonial system in the territory of Nubia. Instead, they allowed the indigenous administration to coexist with the Egyptian one. Egypt was only interested in controlling the religious centers and the elite, so the substructure of the social life was left in the hands of the local people. This indigenous structure was based on a political system of chiefdoms, and their existence is proved by the lack of Egyptian funerary customs in the burial sites of the middle and lower social classes.

Because the temple cities were the remnants of Egyptian control over the region, they were the first to collapse once the indigenous political system reemerged. But this doesn't mean the area became depopulated, as it was previously thought. Instead, a new system of smaller political entities emerged. Each individual of the Nubian elite could grab a piece of power for himself and gather followers. They were well educated and had experience in administration, as they were an integral part of the Egyptian rule. A number of these elites grabbed control of an area and started their own states, known as the successor states to the Egyptian rule in Nubia.

Even though the leading elite had experience in administration, they did not manage to keep the same level of economic and social organization structures. In fact, the successor states relapsed into less-developed societies, relying on limited local resources. At the same time, literacy levels dropped, as the Egyptian professional class left the region. This lack of literacy caused a relapse to primitive forms of the political administration.

The fragmented successor states couldn't survive on their own, as some controlled the fertile lands that could feed the population, while others controlled the gold mines. But each was a victim of constant attacks by the various neighboring tribes, which saw an opportunity to assert their own control in the region. It seems that the unification of the successor states was necessary in order for the Kushites to survive. Egypt continued its efforts to impose control over Nubia once again, and its military campaigns were the perfect political background for Nubian unification.

In the region between the Fourth and Fifth Cataracts of the Nile, the El-Kurru chiefdom controlled the gold mines. But it wasn't only the gold mines that gave this chiefdom an advantage. Geographically, their territory was right on the caravan route between Abu Hamed, which was an important trade center, and Lower Nubia. They also had access to roads that led to Butana and farther into the deep interior of the African continent.

El-Kurru is a large necropolis that was discovered near today's Kurru village. Under this village, there lies the whole ancient city of El-Kurru; however, it remains unexcavated because of its location directly under the living village. The necropolis used to be the main burial place of the Egyptian Twenty-Fifth Dynasty, which was founded by the Kushite rulers. However, some of the remains discovered suggest that kings from as early as the Eighteenth and Nineteenth Dynasties were buried here.

After the end of Egypt's dominion over the region, it seems that El-Kurru took over the role of the capital city, which used to belong to the Egyptian Napata (15 kilometers, or nine miles, to the north of El-Kurru). Egyptian sources mention that Karoy was the southernmost city under their control, so perhaps they were referring to El-Kurru. The form Kurru was either derived from the Egyptian Karoy or had completely indigenous origins.

The burial places of the El-Kurru necropolis that were dated to the earliest periods of Egyptian rule contain no Egyptized features. These purely indigenous mortuary rites strongly resemble the Kerma C-group culture. The items found were dated to various years between 2200 and 1550 BCE. This proves that the indigenous social system coexisted with the Egyptians during the centuries of their dominion. The bodies discovered in the earliest tombs were positioned on beds, which was the practice of the Kerma culture before its fall under

Egypt. Later tombs display a profound turn toward the Egyptian culture. The change was religious as well as archaeological, as the tombs changed shapes and cult practices. More and more Egyptian items were found in the niches around the main tomb, and there was no bed for the body of the deceased. Tombs became sacral places tightly bound to the cult of worshiping the ruler. As such, they were closed, and people had no access to them.

The first name that appears in the written sources of Egypt, as well as in the tomb in El-Kurru, is Alara. He is believed to be the first prince and the founder of the dynasty that would rule not only the Kingdom of Kush but also start the Twenty-Fifth Dynasty of Egypt. His name was first discovered on a stela dedicated to his daughter, Queen Tabiry, the wife of Piye (747–716 BCE).

Even though Alara's name is written without a title on Tabiry's stelae, he is mentioned in the royal ring (cartouche); therefore, he was given royal status. It seems that his reign was very long, as later kings would make a reference of wishing their reign was as long as that of Alara's. Traditionally, his reign is considered to be between 780 and 760 BCE; however, there is no strong evidence to confirm this. Later written sources give him various titles, and it is hard to discern if these were used to prove the legitimacy of the dynasty or were his actual titles. He is referred to as both "chieftain" and "king." In one of the inscriptions found at the temple in Kawa, he even carries the title "son of Re."

Alara renewed the importance of the city of Napata as the religious center. There, the temple of Amun-Re functioned during his rule, and his sister was ordained in that temple. This is clearly the sign of the El-Kurru chiefdom turning toward and fully accepting Egyptian religion. They established the cult of Amun and the concept of this god as the source of royal power. The sources found in Kawa also mention that Alara had to fight off opponents who challenged his legitimacy and the Egyptianization of the chiefdom. But Alara found powerful ideology in the Egyptian religion, as it helped him establish himself as the ultimate ruler. It was this ideology that allowed him to create a new socio-economic structure and form the Kingdom of Kush.

Chapter 2 – From Alara to the Twenty-Fifth Dynasty

Alara was succeeded by Kashta, who was probably his brother. The written evidence is insufficient to claim the relationship between the two kings, and even their regnal years remain unknown. But there is strong evidence that Kashta was the father of the next king: Piye. Since we know Piye ruled from 747 to 716 BCE, we can hypothesize the ruling years of the previous two kings. It is believed that Alara ruled somewhere between 780 and 860 and Kashta between 760 and 747/4 BCE.

During the reign of Kashta, the authority of the Kingdom of Kush extended from the Butana region in the south to Lower Nubia in the north. This suggests that the kingdom was already a very complex state. The Egyptian religion was already adopted, and the official Nubian cult of Amun was established. Both Alara and Kashta most likely married their sisters, but this is debatable. It is possible the marriages, if they even took place, were of a sacred nature. Alara elevated his sister to the position of a priestess of Amun to create a system of royal succession and to implement the idea of rulers being divine in the minds of the people. This way, the Kushite tradition of succession was similar to the already existing Egyptian one. With it came the concept of kingship and the role of a sister, who was the bride of Amun. Since Amun was a symbol of kingship, it is easy to mistake the marriage to Amun with a marriage to the king.

However, the question remains: why did the Kushites go back to Egyptian traditions after enjoying centuries of independence? The simplest answer lies in the geographical position of the newly established Kingdom of Kush. Since it lay on very important trade routes and produced much gold, Egypt was constantly interested in Kush. Scholars theorize that by allowing Egyptianization once more, the Kushite kings avoided being conquered directly. Through careful diplomacy, they managed to keep their independence, even if it meant adopting their northern neighbor's cultural and religious practices. Trade agreements brought about numerous Egyptian items for everyday use in Kushite lives. This meant the Kush had constant contact with Thebes, from which it slowly adopted the Egyptian religion and the cult of Amun.

Egypt continued to consider Nubia its tributary state, and some conflict occurred, as they expected a yearly tribute payment. When the Kushite kings failed to deliver, the Egyptians would send military expeditions to seize the expected tribute. Egypt even kept the title of viceroy of Kush until 750 BCE, even though it wasn't a formal office. It was, in fact, limited to administering the areas of Lower Nubia, such as Thebes and Elephantine. But the disappearance of the viceregal office came about during the rule of King Kashta. The stela found in the Khnum (or Chnum) temple describes Kashta as the "King of Upper and Lower Egypt" and "Son of Re, Lord of Two Lands." The name Kashta can be translated as "The Kushite," and it is quite probable the king adopted this name once he started ruling in Egypt.

But what happened to the Egyptian rulers, and how did the king of Kush take over the rule seemingly without effort? Since the middle of the 8th century, Egypt underwent a process of fragmentation. Even though the official ruler was Smendes's Twenty-First Dynasty

(1077/1076–1052 BCE), High Priest of Amun Herihor's descendants rose to power as the regents of Middle and Upper Egypt. Since each party had its own followers, the kingdom was divided between the pharaoh and the high priests, who also took royal titles in order to rule the lands. To mend the wounds of the political divide, the royal family agreed to transfer power to Libyan chiefs through official marriages. The Twenty-Second Dynasty was founded by the Libyan men who possessed high-ranking offices in the Egyptian court and were allowed to marry into the royal family.

Even though nothing changed in the administrative structure of the kingdom, Libyans brought changes to the social structure of the Egyptians. They valued ancestry, descent, and belonging to the clan. These values continued to shake the very foundations of Egypt's centralized bureaucratic system. In fact, over the next two centuries, decentralization became a type of government. The clans or leading families were given much more political influence, and individuals started rising to power, especially in Lower Egypt. The Western Delta of the Nile was dominated by the Libyan chiefs as well, while the Eastern Delta belonged to the remaining two branches of the Twenty-Second Dynasty's family members.

Even though the state was politically fragmented, it did not fall into chaos. Everyday life for a commoner continued, and the old quarrels with neighbors had to be maintained. In fact, Egypt was based on a model of polyarchy, meaning the different powerful leaders divided the rule between themselves. With it, the administration was divided, diminishing the centralized state. But the fragmentation didn't bother Egypt's economy. It seems that decentralization allowed each region to develop separately from the others, and the economy thrived everywhere.

However, this system of polyarchy couldn't last for long. Sooner or later, there would be an individual wanting all the power for himself. In around 836 BCE, the remaining members of the Twenty-Second Dynasty were expelled from Thebes, where they ruled, and the Twenty-Third Dynasty started a civil war. Through conflict, they gained full control of Upper Egypt. To secure the legitimacy of the new royal line, they installed Shepenwepet I, the daughter of Pharaoh Osorkon III, as the God's Wife of Amun. This title would prove to be very important for the peaceful transition of Egypt into the hands of the Kushite kings.

To keep the ideology of national unity, even during the time of the division of Egypt into a polyarchy, the new office of Divine Adoratrice of God's Wife of Amun of Thebes was introduced. People needed to believe that the kingship was still sacred and that the unity of the whole nation came from the coexistence and coregency of the god Amun, the pharaoh, and the high priest. The installation of the God's Wife had a purpose of legitimizing the succession, as she was seen as the mother of the king, who was the son of a god. The title of God's Wife of Amun was reserved for the royal princess, and she would take up the role of the main priestess of the Amun cult. The title brought legitimacy to her family, as well as to the control over Thebes and its surroundings.

Shepenwepet I was the only "God's Wife of Amun of Thebes" who was also a ruler. She controlled all of Upper Egypt, which was considered the realm of Amun. Instead of settling for the non-ruling title of queen, she adopted the names "Lord of Two Lands" and "Lord of Appearances." But due to the diplomatic relations, Shepenwepet had to adopt the daughter of a Kushite king into her office of God's Wife. Amenirdis, the daughter of King Kashta, became the presumptive Divine Adoratrice, the one who would inherit the titles from Shepenwepet I. This diplomatic tactic secured Kashta with the means to take over the territories in Egypt without open conflict.

There is no written or archaeological evidence that proves there were violent conflict moments before Kashta's takeover of Egypt. In fact, there is more evidence to support the theory of a peaceful transition to Kushite rule. The descendants of Pharaoh Osorkon III, Takelot III, and Rudamun continued to live freely in Thebes. Even more, they were of high social status, and once they died, they were buried with honors. If they were the enemies of Kashta, the Kushite king would not allow them any honors. The members of the Twenty-Third Dynasty continued to live and prosper peacefully under the Kushite rule. This can only be explained by the decision Rudamun made, which was to withdraw from Thebes to Heracleopolis and rule there, even if this city was already under the control of Thebes.

All of the evidence supports the idea of a peaceful transition of the rule. The previous ruler retreated without conflict, securing his family members' high social status. The installation of Amenirdis I as the Divine Adoratrice may have been just a formality to legitimize this transition of power, but it may also have started it. But what actually triggered the Egyptian rulers to hand down all their power to the Kushite king? There is a hypothesis that Egypt faced a serious threat from their western neighbors, the Libyan chiefs, who sought to extend their territories. However, to the south of Egypt, a new force came to power: the Kingdom of Kush. Egypt was suddenly in between two potential invaders, and its only solution was to turn to the more peaceful neighbor as an ally. Egypt made the alliance with the Kingdom of Kush in order to fight off the Libyans. But the price was very high, as it cost the Egyptians their kingdom.

To support this hypothesis, there are remains of Kushite garrisons in Egypt that date from Kashta's reign. They were positioned to protect Egypt from an attack from the west. After the danger passed, they continued to function, probably to assert Kashta's authority in the region. It seems that it wasn't the pharaohs of the Twenty-Third Dynasty who came up with the idea of handing the rule over to the Kushites. It was the powerful priesthood of Amun who saw it as the only solution to the country's problem, and they forced it upon their kings. To promote Kashta as a ruler, he was given the title "The Possessor of Truth," which was modeled on the Twelfth Dynasty, the dynasty that restored order to the state. By bearing their titles, the priesthood wanted to make a connection between the king of Kush and order, which would please the people of Egypt. Kashta was now represented as the king who would bring peace and prosperity to his subjects, and thus, the transition of power was smooth.

Whatever written sources we have that date from the period of Kashta's rule are not enough to gain an insight into what the political and social systems of both Kush and Egypt were like. Even in Napata, the remains that date to this period remain unexcavated. We can only hazard a guess that it was the political contacts Kashta had with Egypt before he became pharaoh that brought about the quick Egyptianization of the Kushite elite families. The newly created necropolis in Butana (the southern regions of Kush) offers evidence for the switch to Egyptian culture. The archaeological remains also prove the introduction of the Egyptian tradition of coffin burials. The many Egyptian items found in the necropolis likewise speak as proof of the adoption of Egyptianized mortuary rights.

These changes were also introduced to the old necropolis at El-Kurru. However, in El-Kurru, we can find even more proof of quick Egyptianization. The temples built for the newly introduced cults were in the Egyptian style, and they employed the professional personnel of the Theban Amun cult temples. The newly established temples became cultural centers from which the Egyptianization of native cults spread over the Kingdom of Kush. They brought Egyptian scripture to the Kushites, which became the main means of articulation for the ideology of kingship and religion. The progressive Egyptianization of the Kingdom of Kush doesn't necessarily mean a quick end of the native culture. In fact, the indigenous structures and items were tolerated, and the two cultures peacefully coexisted for quite some time.

King Piye (747-716 BCE)

King Kashta died in around 747 and was buried in El-Kurru, according to the Egyptian traditions. He was succeeded by Piye, who continued the Kushite policy of Egyptianization. The new king assumed the titles that belonged to Pharaoh Thutmose III of the Eighteenth Dynasty (1479-1425 BCE). He did this in order to bind himself to the already known system of Egyptian kingship and to prepare the society for a change, as he decided to move his capital from Thebes to Napata. This is strongly suggested by the title Thutmose III assumed, "The Strong Bull Appearing in Thebes," which Piye changed to "The Strong Bull Appearing in Napata."

Another symbolic reason for adopting the titles that belonged to Thutmose III is that this particular pharaoh managed to conquer the lands of Kush during his last regnal years. And now, Piye was the one who was conquering Egypt.

In Piye's third regnal year, a monument with a very important inscription was erected in Napata. It is known as the Sandstone Stela of the Amun temple, and it contains the king's speech, in which he pronounces himself a legitimate ruler of Egypt and the overlord of all the princes and chiefs who occupied his state. He acknowledged the sacred need of tradition to expand the lands he ruled, but he also accepted the status quo of Egypt's contemporary political scene. Egypt was ruled by various chiefs, and Piye was willing to tolerate them as long as they acknowledged his supremacy and paid him tribute.

In his fourth regnal year, Piye traveled to Thebes to bring the offerings to a god, probably Amun. There, he took part in the Opet ritual, which was performed to renew someone's rule. Since Piye did this ritual in the presence of his army, it is presumed he was in conflict with some of the Theban rulers and that he ended this conflict with a victory. It is also possible that Piye came to help defend Thebes, which was under attack by the western chiefs who sought to expand their territories. It is already known that the enemy of Thebes at that time was Osorkon of Sais, who started expanding his domain of influence in 750 BCE.

There are no records of Piye for the next fifteen years, so it is not known how the Kushite king reacted to the Assyrian threat on Lower Egypt from 744 until 732 BCE. At that time, Neo-Assyrian ruler Tiglath-Pileser III conquered almost the whole known world, reaching as far as Gaza, where he appointed a chief, Idibi'ilu of an Arab tribe, to the position of "Gatekeeper of Egypt." This appointment was a sign that the Assyrian king recognized Egypt as a threat and that his vassals were ready to defend Assyrian interest in Palestine. However, no Egyptian sources survive to inform us of Piye's reaction to these events.

It seems that Piye's double kingdom (Kush and Middle Egypt) went through a series of changes that strengthened military, economic, and social power. The cultural integration between the two halves of the kingdom continued undisrupted, and Kush went on with its intention to accept all aspects of the Egyptian culture, from religion and mortuary rights to art, literacy, and everyday life. The kingdom was politically very stable and was ready to face the coalition that rose in the west of Egypt. There, Tefnakht, Prince of Sais, gathered allies and proclaimed himself the "Great Chief of the West." Tefnakht took over Memphis, which Piye did not protest. In fact, Piye recognized the domain of the western prince until he learned about the coalition between Tefnakht of Sais and the king of Hermopolis. Their plan was to attack Heracleopolis, a city that stood between Piye's Middle Egypt and the Western Delta.

Taking this city would be a direct threat to Piye's rule, and even though he didn't react when the coalition forces took over Heracleopolis, he couldn't allow them to subdue the chiefs of the surrounding areas, as this would give them too much power. To stop them, Piye sent the Kushite army stationed in Thebes to attack Hermopolis, where Nimlot ruled. The two armies first clashed at Heracleopolis, in which Tefnakht lost the battle and retired to Hermopolis. Then the Kushites besieged the city, and Piye took over personal control of his army.

Nimlot of Hermopolis surrendered, and Piye managed to enter the city in triumph. There, he received the surrender of local chiefs, whose territories opened the way to Memphis. After a brief siege, Memphis also fell, and Piye's reign was confirmed there in the sanctuary of the god Ptah. Again, more local chiefs came to submit to the Kushite king, among them the hereditary prince of Heliopolis, Peteese. Yet again, his kingship had to be reaffirmed, this time in the sanctuary of Re in Heliopolis. This means that Piye's rule was affirmed by the three major gods of Egypt: Amun, Ptah, and Re. As he progressed toward the east, more chiefs submitted to his rule; according to the written sources, there was a total of fifteen. Among them were the descendants of the previous rulers, such as Iuput II of the Twenty-Third Dynasty, whose ancestors ruled Leontopolis.

Tefnakht fled Memphis before Piye captured it, and he found shelter in the Northern Delta of the Nile. He sent a diplomatic envoy to negotiate with the Kushite king, through whom he recognized Piye as overlord. However, his surrender was only temporary. Tefnakht managed to retain independence for his region in the Western Delta, and as soon as Piye left northern Egypt for Napata, he assumed a royal title, calling himself King Shepsesre Tefnakht I.

Piye conquered the northern parts of Egypt, but he didn't set up his own administration there. Instead, he reinstalled the rulers in the conquered cities who swore allegiance to him: Iuput II in Leontopolis, Peftjauawybast in Heracleopolis, Osorkon II in Tanis, and Nimlot in Hermopolis. Piye erected the Triumph Stela to celebrate his conquest, and according to the written text, he only allowed Nimlot to enter his palace and speak with the king. The other three rulers were considered impure, for the stela describes them as uncircumcised and fish-eaters. This means they were religiously impure and unable to see the face of the pharaoh because they belonged to the line of Libyan chiefs.

Piye's supreme kingship in Egypt was confirmed by three different deities, and the unification of the north and south of the kingdom occurred. The Kushite king now took the title of "King of Upper and Lower Egypt." As such, he was the founder of the Twenty-Fifth Dynasty. His descendants would continue the rule over the united double kingdoms of Kush and Egypt. But there is no evidence that Piye ever visited northern Egypt again. It seems he remained in Napata while leaving the administration of Thebes to God's Wife Amenirdis I, who now adopted Piye's daughter, Shepenwepet II, as the future Divine Adoratrice.

When King Piye died, his remains were transferred to the royal tomb in El-Kurru. He was buried in the first Egyptian pyramid built in this region, and its style was based on the pyramids of the New Kingdom and the pyramids of previous viceroys of Kush. It had very steep sides, and the burial niche closely follows all of the Egyptian mortuary rights. It is safe to presume that by the time Piye died, the Egyptianization of Kush was completed.

Chapter 3 – The Rulers of the Twenty-Fifth Dynasty

Shebitqo and Shabaqo

Surviving Portrait of Shebitqo
https://en.wikipedia.org/wiki/Shebitku#/media/
File:Shabatka_portrait,_Aswan_Nubian_museum.jpg

By the year 720 BCE, Assyria, under the rule of Sargon II, conquered Samaria and Transjordania and was approaching the Nile Delta, where Piye's rule was almost at an end. King Osorkon IV of Tanis was under an immediate threat of an Assyrian invasion, as their army was stationed only 120 miles from Tanis. Osorkon IV was forced to send gifts to Sargon II and try the diplomatic way of preserving his rule. Piye died in 716 BCE, leaving the double kingdom in the hands of his successor: Shebitqo (716-702 BCE). However, the kingdom was again facing turmoil, as the Tefnakht's descendant, Bakenranef, continued the ambitious policy of expanding the territory of Sais. The only way to deal with the increasing tensions in the north was to move the capital from Kush's Napata to Egypt's Memphis.

However, it turned out that Bakenranef wasn't difficult to deal with. Shebitqo managed to crush his forces and kill the king of Sais within the first two years of his reign. In the next four years, the Kushite king managed to capture all of Sais, as well as the region of Pharbaitos, where he restored the security of the kingdom's border. Although the Kushite kings were leaning toward the old centralized government of Egypt, they realized the dangers the kingdom fragmenting if any of the local dynasties happened to grab too much power. This is why the Kushite pharaohs decided to allow local dynasties to exist under the authority of a governor.

At this point, Shebitqo only had to deal with Assyria, and it seems he was lucky in that political field too. In around 712 BCE, Iamani, the ruler of Ashdod (a city in Israel), rebelled against Sargon II, and it seems he wanted Egypt's collaboration. To negotiate the possible alliance with Shebitqo, Iamani sent him gifts. However, the alliance never occurred, and the Kushite king never sent military help to Ashdod. Instead, Iamani fled once the Assyrians approached, and he was received as an asylum seeker in Shebitqo's court. There, he stayed for some time, but as soon as Assyria represented a serious threat to Egypt, Shebitqo extradited Imani to preserve the good relations with the superior empire. But there is some evidence that supports the hypothesis that during Imani's time at Shebitqo's court, it was Shebitqo's successor, Shabaqo, who delivered the ruler of Ashdod to Sargon II.

Now that the double kingdom had entered a period of peace, Shebitqo concentrated on the neglected Egyptian royal custom of building temples. However, his goal wasn't only to culturally and religiously enrich his state. He wanted to consolidate the Twenty-Fifth Dynasty's power over the kingdom through the installation of royal cults all over the country. The dynasty already had its legitimacy guaranteed by the God's Wife of Amun, Shepenwepet II, but Shebitqo felt the need to elevate his own son, Haremakhet, to the position of High Priest of Amun of Thebes. This title had fallen into oblivion half a century earlier, and through the installation of the pharaoh's son, it was resurrected and made hereditary. It is possible that Shebitqo had no daughters to elevate to the position of Divine Adoratrice, and to confirm the legitimacy of his rule, he reopened the institution of the High Priest of Amun.

Shebitqo also needed to confirm his legitimacy because he succeeded Piye according to the Kushite collateral succession rights, as he was more than likely the brother of the previous king. But this wasn't the patrilineal succession model recognized in Egypt, and therefore, he needed to legitimize his kingship. In the next years of Shebitqo's rule, he introduced Kushite priests to Thebes. The new appointments, such as the Fourth Prophet of Amun and Mayor of Thebes, allowed Kushite dignitaries to enter the high social circles of Egypt. Intermarriages naturally followed, and Thebes became the center of Nubian and Egyptian social life.

Although Shebitqo moved the capital to Memphis, temple building didn't occur there. This is probably because the move was pushed by military needs. But something else was happening in this city on a cultural scale. As a new capital, Memphis needed to be connected to the kingship, and thus, new myths about the region were created. Memphis was now seen as the birthplace of the pharaohs and the original place of the creation of the whole world. The Shabaqo Stone, an Egyptian relic from Memphis, describes the creation of the world by the god Ptah. As a patron of artists and craftsmen, Ptah was the ultimate creator who crafted the whole universe and life in it. This part of the text of the Shabaqo Stone is known as the "Memphite Theology."

Shebitqo died in his new capital after fifteen years of rule. Like his predecessors, he was buried at El-Kurru in the Kingdom of Kush. His successor was his son, Shabaqo (702–690 BCE), who is famous for his clash with the Assyrian Empire. It occurred shortly after the new king's coronation. The army of Kush was summoned and placed under the command of Taharqo, who would succeed Shabaqo. It is speculated that the new king had no male offspring, so he decided to elevate Taharqo to the position of his heir apparent. The Egyptian tradition says the crown prince was to take control of the kingdom's expeditionary army, and Shabaqo proclaimed him the commander-in-chief accordingly.

By 704 and 703 BCE, a coalition between the Phoenicians and Philistines against the Assyrian Empire already existed, and it seems Shabaqo decided to support this alliance. He sent his army to meet the forces of Sennacherib, the successor of Sargon II. The battle occurred probably around 701 BCE at Eltekeh (Israel), and the Egyptian-Kushites, under the leadership of their crown prince, were beaten. However, this battle could be interpreted as an Egyptian-Kushite victory even though the army was destroyed. This is due to the fact that Sennacherib retreated to Philistia after this battle, and Shabaqo continued to peacefully rule until the end of his days.

Scholars couldn't agree for quite some time whether Shabaqo or Shebitqo ruled first. This is because the carbon-dating of the items belonging to the two kings gave approximately the same results. After all, they ruled in a short span of time. So, scholars had to turn to written sources to solve this dilemma. In the past, it was believed that Shabaqo ruled before Shebitqo; however, modern findings seem to favor the opposite theory. One of these findings is the depiction of Shepenwepet I, God's Wife of Amun, performing the religious rites in the Amun temple. This depiction was created during the rule of Shebitqo, while the ones with similar scenes that contain the rites performed by Amenirdis I were created during the rule of Shabaqo. From the textual evidence, we know Shepenwepet I was the God's Wife of Amun before Amenirdis; therefore, it is only logical to conclude that Shebitqo ruled before Shabaqo.

Another piece of evidence that would speak in favor of the Shebitqo-Shabaqo rule is the shape of the tombs they were buried in. While they are stylistically common for Egypt of that period, the one in which Shebitqo was buried looks closer to the tomb of Piye. Shabaqo's tomb, on the other hand, looks much like Taharqo's, the tomb of his successor. This is a clear indication that the styles changed over time, and within just a few generations, the differences could be seen.

Taharqo

Taharqo depicted as a sphinx
https://upload.wikimedia.org/wikipedia/commons/
2/2e/SphinxOfTaharqa.jpg

Like his predecessors of Kushite origin, Shabaqo was buried in El-Kurru. Taharqo became the king of the double kingdom, and he was crowned in Memphis in 690 BCE. As his predecessors had no male hairs of mature age, Taharqo, the son of Piye, was chosen to rule. In Egypt, it wasn't unheard of to have a child pharaoh, and Shabaqo did have a younger brother named Tanwetamani (Tantamani) who he could have installed as the heir apparent instead of Taharqo. However, it seems the immediate danger of a war with the Assyrian Empire led to the decision of a mature prince taking the throne. At the time, Tanwetamani was just an infant, and he couldn't lead the army. Also, Taharqo was the son of Piye, a king who had united the north and south of the Egyptian kingdom.

In the first seventeen years, Taharqo ruled in peace, and he was able to bring prosperity to the double kingdom. Trade continued to bloom, and the economy got stronger. The construction of new temples was the main cultural occupation of the kingdom at the time, and they were erected both in Kush and Egypt. But all the building activities were concentrated in the cities, which were the administrative centers of the region. This means the new king sought to consolidate a centralized government. The scale of the building projects in Memphis and Thebes was monumental. Even timber, such as cedar, juniper, and acacia, which are of Asian origin, was introduced. This speaks of the possible opening of new trade routes and the economic power of the double kingdom.

Special attention was given to building new temples in Napata, which resembled the old ones in Karnak. The sacred mountain Gebel Barkal, with its ninety-meter high cliffs that hang above the Nile, was perfect for erecting new, curiously shaped temples dedicated to Amun. After all, it was said this god lived at the top of the mountain, and so, it was only natural to build a temple at its foot. There, Taharqo carved a separate small inner chamber that contained his cartouche titles and a text dedicated to a triumph (however, it is unreadable today).

Besides temple building in Napata, Taharqo dedicated the first years of his reign to developing urban centers all over the Kushite territories. These renewed towns in Kush served as local centers of government. They were the production and redistribution points of items, which were sent all over the double kingdom. They had the traditional form of the temple-towns with a newly added socio-economic role based on the temple-towns of the New Kingdom of Egypt. However, Taharqo didn't simply build new towns. Instead, he worked on renewing the existing ones and repopulating those towns that had been abandoned during the reigns of his predecessors.

One of the scripts from Kawa mentioned the Libyan donation of children, servants, and cult items, which indicates Taharqo sent military expeditions to the western border of his kingdom and to the Levant, probably as far as the Phoenician coast. While the donation of Libyan servants is a clear sign of warfare, some of the items on the list might have been diplomatic gifts from the Philistine cities, such as various cultural objects. There are also signs of trade contracts with Assyria, as the sources from Nineveh (an Assyrian city in today's Iraq) mention the importation of the Kushite chariots and horses.

A statue of Pharaoh Taharqo discovered in Karnak has a text engraved on it that lists all of the conquered territories, which are mostly known Asiatic principalities in Egypt, but it also includes a list of conquered peoples, such as Libyans, Shasu nomadic people, and possibly Phoenicians. Egypt probably renewed its presence in the Levant due to Assyria being too busy fighting a war with Babylon. A stela was found on the road between Memphis and Fayoum, which describes how Pharaoh Taharqo ordered its army to practice long-distance running, while he followed his racing soldiers in a chariot. This inscription proves that the king had a close relationship with his army and that he paid close interest in its training and organization. The Twenty-Fifth Dynasty brought about the view that soldiering was a divine profession. The religious connotation given to the army lasted at least as long as the reign of Piye, but it is possible that it was a Kushite tradition brought to Egypt. In the Kushite tradition, the king was seen as an ideal athlete and hero, whose war achievements were unmatched.

The double kingdom under Pharaoh Taharqo finally reached a point where there was no cultural, economic, or social difference between Egypt and Kush. Finally, the Kingdom of Kush was completely integrated into what used to be the norm for the Egyptian centralized government. The de-Egyptianization of the Kushites would be impossible by now, as the people identified as one. The separation of the kingdom would come much later, and it would be done by the Assyrians, whose conquest of Egypt would disassemble the double kingdom and send Kush on its own way.

The burial sites found in southern Kush that have been dated to Taharqo's rule are standing evidence of how far the Egyptianization of the people of Kush went. Although the funerary rituals were similar, they were not the same. This testifies that some form of indigenous culture was preserved, though the use of Egyptian talismans, the positioning of the bodies, and the use of Egyptian face masks are evidence enough that the people identified as the same both in the south of the kingdom and in the north. Still, it was a very heterogeneous society with different groups of people meddling together to create its core.

Taharqo installed his own daughter, Amenirdis II, as the God's Wife of Amun of Thebes, and following the example of his predecessor, he installed his son, Nesi-Shu-Tefnut, as the Second Prophet of Amun (since the position of High Priest was occupied by Haremakhet). However, not all the administrative positions went to members of the royal family. The elite families of Thebes and Memphis occupied such positions as High Steward of the Divine Adoratrice or the Mayor of Thebes. The local dynasties of Lower Egypt continued to assert administrative control over their ancestral territories, but they operated only as delegates of Egypt's central government. This means they were partly independent, but to what extent remains to be discovered.

The first half of Taharqo's reign was peaceful, and the double kingdom prospered. The king did his duty and warred to expand his kingdom because it was seen as a religious obligation of the ruler. But conflict never touched the territories of his realm, and the people themselves were not involved. But in 671 BCE, a new Assyrian invasion began, and Egypt was not safe anymore. It took three battles on the Egyptian frontiers for the Assyrians to finally move inward and take Memphis. The sources notify us that the pharaoh was wounded, but no specific details are given. Taharqo had to flee his capital, probably to the south.

Memphis fell quickly, and the Assyrians didn't even have to besiege it. It was quite odd for the capital to be so weakly defended, especially since the royal family was present. The crown prince, Nes-Anhuret, was taken by the Assyrians, together with some of the royal wives and other members of the household. A stela found in Nineveh testifies that the great treasure was taken from Memphis, including 50,000 horses from the royal stables. The Assyrian ruler Esarhaddon proclaimed himself king in Egypt, even though he captured only some of the territories of Lower Egypt. Still, he received the submission of the local kings, chiefs, and officials, and he even appointed some of his own. The local dynasties became Assyrian vassals.

The years that followed are remembered as the dark years in which foreigners ruled Egypt. The Kushite Twenty-Fifth Dynasty managed to unite Egypt and rule the double kingdom while times were peaceful, but they showed their true inadequacy when confronted by a superior foreign power. Taharqo blamed the gods, saying how Amun had abandoned him before he could finish his rule. In the inscription engraved in the temple of Karnak at around 674 BCE, the pharaoh goes to great lengths to justify his failure. He asks the gods to help him retrieve the lost lands, but at the same time, he also blames them. The whole point of this fragmented text was to secure the legitimacy of the Twenty-Fifth Dynasty and to prove the father-son relationship between Amun and the pharaoh.

Esarhaddon left Egypt and placed Necho I as the king of Sais, who assumed the pharaonic titles. It is possible that the Assyrian ruler gave Memphis to Necho I and that he ruled as a vassal Egyptian pharaoh. However, Taharqo moved quickly, and he instigated some revolts in Lower Egypt as soon as the Assyrian army was gone. In fact, he caused so much trouble that Esarhaddon had to launch a second invasion of Egypt in 669 BCE. But the Assyrian king died of an illness on his way there, and Taharqo managed to capture Memphis back. It remains obscure if the Kushite king retrieved Lower Egypt after Esarhaddon's death or before. Nevertheless, the new Assyrian king, Assurbanipal (669–627 BCE), continued his father's task. He didn't just invade Egypt in 667/666 BCE; he also decided to annex it.

In the battle, which took place near the Eastern Delta of the Nile in 671 BCE, the Egyptian-Kushite army of King Taharqo was defeated. The Kushite king abandoned his troops and fled to Thebes. But he was pursued by the Assyrian army, which had help from the kingdoms of the Nile's Delta, as Assurbanipal received the submission of all the local dynasties between Memphis and Thebes. This discouraged Taharqo, who had to retreat even farther south. The Assyrians even received the full submission of the mayor of Thebes, who was apparently trying to preserve the city and stop any possible sacking. Satisfied, Assurbanipal returned to Nineveh, leaving Egypt in the hands of vassal rulers who were under the strict supervision of the Assyrian army, which stayed in the region.

But it didn't take long for some of these local rulers to turn against the Assyrians. Around 665 BCE, the princes of Sais, Mendes, and Pelusium turned again toward Kushite King Taharqo, and together, they plotted a rebellion. Unfortunately, word of the rebellion reached Assurbanipal just in time, and all the involved parties were arrested. Taharqo remained in Kush and was beyond the Assyrians' reach. For unknown reasons, Necho of Sais was the only one who wasn't executed. Instead, he was made a vassal ruler of Memphis, while his son Psamtik was given Athribis to rule. It is possible that Sais was strategically important or economically strong, so the Assyrian king decided to become politically involved in its dynasty. Psamtik would later be the founder of the Twenty-Sixth Dynasty, an opportunity he grasped from his appointment as the king of Athribis, a city where the heir presumptive was usually appointed by pharaohs before their installation as rulers.

Taharqo died in Kush in 664 BCE without the opportunity to regain Egypt as the second half of the double kingdom. Unlike his predecessors, he wasn't buried in El-Kurru. He founded a new necropolis in Nuri, just opposite of Napata.

The End of Kushite Rule in Egypt

Taharqo was succeeded by his cousin, the younger brother of Shabaqo: Tanwetamani. This succession wasn't patrilineal like the Egyptian tradition demanded, but it is possible that the new ruler was installed by the military and that the political situation in the kingdom led to this collateral succession, which was practiced in Kush. Tanwetamani was born around 702 BCE, which means he was around thirty-eight when his predecessor died. His age and reputation gave him the boost he needed among the soldiers to succeed Taharqo instead of his own son, the young prince Atlanersa.

After the coronation and recognition as the Son of Amun, Tanwetamani gathered his army and sailed to Thebes. On his way, he made a stop in Elephantine, where his rule was confirmed by the god Khnum. He took Thebes, and he performed a ritual there that granted him recognition as the king of Egypt who had been installed by Amun himself. As if this wasn't enough, the new pharaoh continued to Karnak, where his rule was again confirmed by Amun. Only then did Tanwetamani feel ready enough to begin retaking the Egyptian territories from the hands of the Assyrians.

The first victory for the new Kushite pharaoh was in Memphis, a city he took without much opposition. It seems that at least there, he had the support of the citizens and the city dignitaries. Nevertheless, he sent a rich war booty to Napata as a sign of victory, even though the transition of power was peaceful. After continuing on to Sais, he had to engage in a battle against Necho. Tanwetamani was victorious, and

Necho, King of Sais, died. The fall of Sais was enough for some of the local dynasties of the Delta to surrender. The Kushite king promised they could keep administering their ancestral territories as long as they recognized him as the overlord. However, not the whole Delta was defeated, and the son of Necho, Psamtik, managed to escape to Assyria.

Assurbanipal received the news of the fall of Memphis and the death of Necho. He made a decision to launch yet another attack on Egypt, and the expedition was ready in 664 BCE. Once the Assyrians arrived, Tanwetamani decided he wasn't strong enough to fight them, and he fled south to Thebes. The abandoned dynasties of the Delta had no other choice but to renew their vassal status with Assyria. But like his predecessor, Tanwetamani was continually chased by the enemy's army, and he had to leave Thebes and run to Kush. But the mayor of Thebes didn't manage to save the city this time. The ransacking and burning of the city of Amun took place, and it shocked the Egyptians. They saw it as a bad omen, and they finally realized their society was fragile and vulnerable. It was the fall of Thebes that eclipsed any further efforts to regain Egypt, and so, the ideology of Amun's direct kingship over Egypt started disappearing. The first split of the double kingdom happened. While Egypt abandoned the idea of Amun as the ultimate ruler, he continued to be the central figure in the Kushite cosmic order.

The Assyrians decided to install Psamtik I as the sole ruler of Egypt, and he started the Twenty-Sixth Dynasty in 664 BCE. To avoid vassal kings swearing allegiance to Kush at the first sign of trouble, the old dynasties were reinstalled, such as the dynasty of Nimlot in Hermopolis and Peftjauawybast in Heracleopolis. Even though Psamtik I was installed by Assurbanipal himself, in the course of the next nine years, he expelled the Assyrian army from Egypt and started ruling independently. In 656 BCE, he installed his daughter, Nitocris, as the God's Wife of Amun Elect, which gave legitimacy to his rule, just as it did to the previous Kushite kings.

However, Upper Egypt remained loyal to Tanwetamani, even though there is evidence that he never returned to these territories again. The political and economic power in Upper Egypt belonged to the Fourth Prophet of Amun and Mayor of Thebes Montuemhat. He was mentioned in inscriptions as the "Prince of Thebes." It was Montuemhat who negotiated with Psamtik I about the installation of his daughter as the God's Wife of Amun. All he asked in return was political immunity for both of her predecessors, Shepenwepet II and Amenirdis II. Nitocris was elevated to the sacred position, and the legitimacy of the dynasty passed from Kashta to Psamtik I. Egypt was lost to the rulers of Kush, and the double kingdom was no more. However, the Kushite court remained closely tied to the Theban clergy of Amun, as their ideology still depended on Egyptian culture. Even though the territorial division of the double kingdom occurred, culturally, the Kush remained Egyptianized and did not revert to its previous indigenous civilization.

Chapter 4 – Relations between Kush and Egypt Continue

Psamtik I began his regnal year in 664 BCE, and after the elevation of his daughter, Nitocris, to the position of Divine Adoratrice Elect, he asserted his authority over Lower Egypt. This means that by 656 BCE, Psamtik unified Egypt under one rule. But he would not have been able to do so if he did not receive the help of local dynasties. To gain the people's trust, he needed to form alliances with the local rulers and wealthy families of Thebes. Because of this, the office of Mayor of Thebes remained in the hands of Kushite Montuemhat, and the nephew of Tanwetamani, Harkhebi, remained the High Priest of Amun.

Since Kushite officials remained in Thebes, Kush remained in contact with Egypt. The nature of this relation was religious at its core, but it influenced other aspects of the Kushite life. Some of the Theban mortuary texts were found in the tombs of the new necropolis in Napata, such as excerpts from the *Book of the Dead*, especially the *Book of Gates* (Egyptian religious texts for the dead). Amun remained the main deity of kingship in Kush, and since his temple in Thebes was traditionally the place where the kingship starts, Kush was unwilling to cut all ties with it. The direct contact between the priesthood of Napata and Thebes had to be maintained.

But the relation between Egypt and the Kingdom of Kush didn't end with their religious bonds. In fact, international trade was of importance for both kingdoms, and Psamtik I encouraged it vigorously. The trade between the two kingdoms continued to bloom during the reign of Psamtik's successor, Necho II, who dug the Red Sea canal to create a new route to the Land of Punt. To assert control over the trade routes along the Nile Valley, Necho had to appease the Troglodytes, nomadic tribes whose territory spread from the Lower Nubian banks of the Nile to the Red Sea.

There is no evidence of the Nubian importation of goods to Egypt during this period, but there were plenty of Egyptian items exported to Kush. These were not just trade goods but also diplomatic gifts, which testify of the efforts to keep peaceful relations between the two kingdoms. These gifts were often in the form of luxury metal vessels, amulets, and furniture. They were found in the burial places of Nuri, where the descendants of the Twenty-Fifth Dynasty were laid to rest.

The decades following Tanwetamani's withdrawal from Egypt saw the Kushites building up their kingdom. The kings who followed had no access to Egyptian building materials, but that didn't stop them from trying to maintain the adopted architecture in Lower Nubia. The kings of the Twenty-Fifth Dynasty kept the high intellectual, artistic, and technical standards of their predecessors who had ruled Egypt. The architecture, arts, and the inscriptions testify to the unbroken continuity of the Egyptian ideology, both religious and political.

A radical change in Egypt's attitude toward Kush occurred during the reign of Psamtik II (595–589 BCE). He organized a military expedition to Kush, which reached Napata. While the cause of this military attack is unknown, there is evidence of the purposeful destruction of monuments, statues, and names of Twenty-Fifth Dynasty kings, both in Kush and in Egypt. This animosity of Egypt would push the Kingdom of Kush toward the south, away from Egyptian influence.

The practice of destroying every memory of the previous rulers is known as *damnatio memoriae* in Latin, and it served the purpose of political propaganda. For some reason, the current rulers saw it as necessary to distance their kingdom from the Kushite rulers of Egypt. Unfortunately, the real reason behind this particular practice of *damnatio memoriae* is unknown. Scholars speculate that it might have been the political tendencies of the Theban Amun priesthood that sparked it. They preserved a positive view on Kush and kept the relations between the two kingdoms alive. They possibly schemed to bring back the Kushite rule, and the descendants of Psamtik I had to react strongly to preserve their legitimacy.

Over the next few decades, the relations between Egypt and the Kingdom of Kush would remain hostile. However, the cultural similarity of the two civilizations continued. The Kushite kings continued erecting their own statues in the Egyptian style. Instead of building them in Thebes or Memphis, they switched to Napata. However, they chose the archaic style of the New Kingdom; thus, these Kushite statues remained uninfluenced by Egypt's contemporary art trends. This was probably due to the isolation of Kush. With the relations between the two kingdoms turning violent, it is no wonder that the Egyptian influence stopped—at least for the moment.

The isolation Kush experienced after the war with Psamtik II was finally lifted during the reign of Pharaoh Ahmose II (570-526 BCE). This renewed contact brought back the international trade between the two neighboring kingdoms, and new Egyptian items were imported to Kush. There is also a document that speaks of a military escort for a trade caravan traveling south through the Nile Valley. The document uses the date of year 41 of Ahmose's rule, which places it to 529 BCE.

Kushite Kings during the 7ᵗʰ Century

Tanwetamani was succeeded by Atlanersa, the son of Taharqo. It is believed that he was too young to inherit the throne after the death of his father, especially since the reconquest of Egypt was being planned. Not much is known about the politics of the Kingdom of

Kush during the reign of Atlanersa because the written evidence is very sparse. However, some of the most important cultural changes happened during his reign. For example, Taharqo's necropolis of Nuri was again in use after Tanwetamani abandoned it for one whole generation.

Another achievement prescribed to Atlanersa is the building of the temple at the foot of the sacred mountain Gebel Barkal near Napata. This temple is known as B700, and it attests to the survival of the temple-building tradition that had been started by the kings of the Twenty-Fifth Dynasty. The iconography and style of the temple match those of Atlanersa's predecessors who had ruled Egypt. Some scholars believe this represents the constitutional and political integrity of the Kingdom of Kush, which continued using the same ideology even after the breakdown of the double kingdom.

One of the reliefs of Temple B700 shows King Atlanersa in the typical scene of "uniting of the two lands." This relief was originally seen as the coronation rite of the Egyptian pharaohs, and it was never before seen in the Kushite tradition. But now, this scene entered the Kushite royal legitimation practice and became a religious theme. Even though the two kingdoms were physically distant, the cultural integration of Egypt's practices continued.

Except for the temples built by Atlanersa and some of the enthronement texts engraved in them, nothing else was preserved, and so, nothing can even be speculated about the reign of this king. He was buried in Nuri in a granite sarcophagus, whose inscriptions testify to the richness of the Kushite traditions. He was succeeded by Senkamanisken, whose reign is even more obscure. We only know about his existence because some of his statues were found in Napata, Kawa, and Meroe. He ruled approximately between 640 and 620 BCE, and he had two sons, who both inherited the throne after him.

The first son to inherit the Kushite throne after Senkamanisken was Anlamani. The exact dates of his rule are unknown, but he died around 600 BCE. His coronation inscription found at the temple of Kawa is the first mention of the Kushites taking an aggressive stance toward some of the nomadic tribes who inhabited their territory. The text describes how King Anlamani annihilated his enemy's forces during the enthronement ceremony. This passage led scholars to believe that the excursion wasn't military in nature but rather ceremonial. This would mean the conflict between the Kushites and the Blemmyae tribe (ancestors of the Beja people in modern Sudan) was staged for the purposes of the king's coronation. It seems Anlamani's enemy was nothing more than a nomadic tribe living in the Kushite territory.

When Anlamani died, the throne was succeeded by his brother, Aspelta. This suggests that Anlamani's reign was short and that he had no mature son who could inherit. The fact that one of his stelae mentioned how he was elected as king by a group of religious and military leaders proves this succession hypothesis. The textual evidence he left behind is enough to come to the conclusion that the period of kings between Tanwetamani and Aspelta was one of political continuity, without larger conflicts in the government itself.

Another stela dated to Aspelta's time, known as the Banishment Stela, mentioned an internal turmoil within the kingdom, but the details of this turmoil remain hidden. Apparently, in the second year of the new king's reign, a crime occurred in Amun temple in Napata, for which the priests were punished. But the more important fact is that the names and titles of Kings Anlamani and Aspelta were erased from this stela and another one found in the Amun temple of Napata. Even the figure of the king was erased from the Banishment Stela, but it was later restored. Also, the face of the Queen Mother, her names and titles, and the names of all the female ancestors of Aspelta were scratched. It seems that the perpetrator intended to disprove the legitimacy of not only of King Anlamani but also of the whole female succession line.

A similar crime occurred in Meroe, where the king's statue was smashed; due to this act, the inscription on it is forever lost. However, not all the stelae of King Anlamani were destroyed. The Khaliut Stela was later transferred to the Amun temple in Napata, where it replaced the old stela. The efforts of King Aspelta to restore Anlamani's good name shows that he deeply cared about his brother's reign. It is quite possible that the destruction of his predecessor's name and image, as well as those of his female ancestors, had something to do with Aspelta's legitimacy to the throne. It is possible that he didn't have the support of all the people and that there were some rebelling individuals who refused his kingship.

The Banishment Stela describes the punishment of a group of priests who were expelled from the city of Napata and burned alive because they tried to kill an innocent man. If the text of the Banishment Stela can be connected with the erasure of the names of the king's brother and mother, it is quite possible that these priests plotted against the king and were punished for it. However, there is no evidence that can connect the Banishment Stela with the obvious *damnatio memoriae* performed upon Kings Anlamani and Aspelta.

Burning the convicted wasn't a usual punishment in Kush, and it could be a sign of a very severe crime, such as plans to kill the king. The fact that priests were involved leads to the idea that there was political turmoil, as the priests were administrative leaders of the kingdom in addition to their religious position. This is because only the priests received enough education to be elected as government officials. The act of burning the convicted seems to have a ritualistic connotation and is connected with a crime against the god Amun. Since Amun was the personification of kingship, it is easy to conclude that the punished priests tried to overthrow the legitimate king.

Psamtik II and the Nubian Campaign

One of the most important events that occurred during the reign of Kushite King Aspelta is certainly the Egyptian military campaign in Nubia. In 593 BCE, Egyptian Pharaoh Psamtik II led his forces against the Kingdom of Kush. The records of this expedition were found on several stelae across Egypt, but the best-preserved text of the pharaoh's triumph was discovered on the Egyptian-Kushite border at Shellal, near Aswan.

The conflict between Egypt and Kush was initiated by Psamtik II, and he precisely planned it, even down to the battle itself occurring when the waters of the First and Second Cataracts were sailable. The pharaoh planned it this way so he could quickly transport his army to Kush. As soon as the Egyptians arrived at Pnubs, the battle started. Pnubs is often referred to in the Kushite enthronement texts, but its real location is a source of speculation. Some believe it could be identified as Tabo on the island of Argo, while others believe that it was the ancient site of the city of Kerma. However, the Egyptian sources describe this territory as "the hill country of Pnubs," and neither ancient Kerma nor Tabo match this description. A third hypothesis about the location of Pnubs claims that it was the impassable region of the Third Cataract.

Either way, if it is true the battle occurred at the site of the Third Cataract, it means the terrain itself was not suitable for the usage of cavalry, for which the Egyptian military was famous. Nevertheless, the pharaoh ordered an attack and was victorious. The texts describe the enemy fleeing the battlefield, as well as the capture of around 4,000 prisoners. Pnubs was the place of the first and final Egyptian victory against the Kushites during the Nubian campaign, but neither of them mentions the cause of the battle. Only a fragment of the Tanis Stela speaks of a possible Nubian attack on the territories of southern Egypt. According to this source, Psamtik II was in Elephantine when he heard of the Kushites' intentions, and he quickly sent an army to the land of Kush.

After the battle at Pnubs, Psamtik II sacked the northern part of the Kingdom of Kush and probably reached Napata, even though the royal residential city is not mentioned in any of the Egyptian sources. This is why some scholars wonder if Egypt was responsible for Napata's troubles or if it was due to an internal struggle in Kush. After all, why wouldn't any Egyptian source mention such an important detail as the occupation of the capital city of their enemies? But the truth is, many of the mentioned geographical places in Kush remain to be located. The Tanis Stela mentions the royal residency *Trgb*, which could be identified as Napata, as it was often referred to as the royal residence.

Whether the Egyptians sacked Napata or not, Aspelta decided to move his capital to the southern city of Meroe, where he felt safer from any renewed attacks. Psamtik II retreated to Elephantine after the victory, and he didn't even bother to establish his government in the newly conquered areas. This suggests that he had no real intention of conquering the territories of Kush but that he was merely stopping any intention this Nubian kingdom might have had of conquering Egypt. The fact that his army destroyed all memory of the Twenty-Fifth Dynasty, both in Egypt and in Kush, shows that the Nubian campaign was indeed an act of resentment toward the Kushites instead of an attempt to conquer new lands.

Napata continued to exist as a city, and for some time, it still acted as the administrative and economic center of the region, even though the royal residency was transferred to Meroe. However, through time, the region became less and less inhibited. Even agriculture suffered, as the people moved farther south, attracted by the rising economic power of Meroe. Napata, once a strong capital of the kingdom, was reduced to a town, which would be plundered once again many centuries later when the Romans, who were provoked by a Kushite queen, entered the region.

Chapter 5 – Kush between the 6th and 3rd Centuries

The next 150 years after the Nubian campaign lacks archaeological and textual evidence. It creates the illusion of a sudden decline, as nothing is preserved about the ten rulers who followed Aspelta except for their tombs. Even these were constantly plundered, so very little was found that gives an insight into the Kushite-Egyptian relationship. All ten kings, from Aramatelqo to Talakhamani, were buried in the Nuri necropolis near Napata, even though the capital was moved to Meroe. This means the tradition was followed, and the continuity of the politics from the Twenty-Fifth Dynasty onward was preserved. It seems even the succession line was straight, and all the kings belonged to the same royal family.

On average, each of the kings of the 6th and the beginning of the 5th century ruled for fifteen years. The titles these Kushite kings used were the same as all the other descendants of the Twenty-Fifth Dynasty, but the lack of Horus, Nebty, and Golden Horus among the titles is evident. It remains unknown if the lack of these titles was an effort of distancing Kush from the Egyptian-style of kingship, or they are missing simply because the sands of time destroyed the inscriptions of the royal tombs.

During this period, Meroe became an important economic, social, and cultural center of the Kingdom of Kush. The excessive building projects started with King Amaninatakilebte, who ruled in the late 6th century, and it continued through the reigns of his successors, Karkamani and Amaniastbarqo. They all invested in the Amun temple in Meroe. Napata wasn't yet fully abandoned, so the building projects continued there as well, although they were limited to the extension of already existing temples.

During the mid-5th century, the ancient Greek historian Herodotus described the lands of Kush, naming them Aethiopia. But he wasn't the first man to use this term. It was mentioned in Homer's *Iliad* and *Odyssey* as the lands inhabited by the "burned-faced" people. The word Aethiopia itself is a derivative of two Greek words, which can be translated as "burned-face," alluding to the skin color of the people who inhabited certain parts of Africa. But Herodotus was the first to use this term in relation to the Kingdom of Kush. He claimed that he personally traveled to Elephantine, the southernmost Egyptian city that was almost on the border with Aethiopia. According to Herodotus, there were two Aethiopias, one that extended from Elephantine to Meroe and the Utopian Aethiopia farther in the south.

Herodotus explains this Utopian Aethiopia in the far south produced enormous amounts of gold and imported huge elephants into Egypt. He describes the people of this faraway part of Kush as very tall and handsome, and he claims they lived very long. The existence of two Aethiopias can be explained by the fluid frontier of Kush and Egypt. It is possible the various political conflicts of the 5th century moved the border between the two kingdoms, meaning the territory in the north of Kush was often swapped with Egypt.

But why were the Greeks interested in Egypt's southern neighbor in the first place? Why was Herodotus there to witness Aethiopia and write about it? It could be Egypt's stance toward the Kush that brought about the interest of foreigners. Sometime during the rule of Pharaoh Ahmose II (Amasis II, 570–526 BCE), the trade relations between Egypt and Kush were renewed. This means Kushite gold and other trade goods, such as animals and ebony, traveled through Egypt to the Mediterranean world of Greece. There, these items sparked interest in where they came from, and this interest was not only of material nature. Scholars, such as Herodotus, were also interested in the people who inhabited the faraway lands south of Egypt.

When Cambyses (525–522 BCE) of the Achaemenid Empire conquered Egypt and proclaimed himself pharaoh, he continued his military expedition into the lands of Kush. The legend even said that he reached the city of Meroe and that he was the one who named it. But in truth, this traditional story might be the reflection of an earlier conquest of Nubia by Psamtik II. During the rule of Persian King Darius the Great (522–486 BCE), Kush was listed as the vassal state of the Persian Empire in the emperor's "peoples list," a document that lists all the peoples who were subjects of the Achaemenid Empire. Before that, it was only mentioned as the land that gave tribute in ivory for the construction of the palace at Susa. When Xerxes I (486–465 BCE) came to rule Persia, Kush was still on the list of vassal states. The historian Herodotus supports the Persian evidence by describing the Kushite warriors as fighting in Xerxes's army in the Battle of Thermopylae.

As a vassal state of the Persian Empire, the Kingdom of Kush still had its own rulers. The Kushite interest in Egypt was renewed, as the old Twenty-Sixth Dynasty that held resentment toward Kush was now gone. The kingdom was free to renew the relationship with its old trade partner, and the old caravan routes were reopened. However, Egypt was struck by a series of rebellions against Persian rule, starting in 486 BCE, and Kush saw it as an opportunity to take back Lower Nubia. This territory, between the First and Second Cataracts, had been conquered by Psamtik II, and since then, it was never really integrated back into Kush.

But the Kushite rulers took their time preparing the reconquest of Lower Nubia. It seems that the moment wasn't right until the third rebellion against Persian rule, which occurred in 414. At that time, Kush was ruled by Irike-Arnannote (also known as Amanineteyerike, whose exact year of reign is unknown), who succeeded his uncle Talakhamani. This collateral succession might have been inspired by the preparation for a military expedition to Lower Nubia. The sources claim Irike-Arnannote was elected king when he was forty-one years old. Again, the kingship was decided by his mature years and experience in warfare.

Another evidence of his intention to retake the long-lost territories of Nubia was his choice of the royal title. "Re is one whose heart is beautiful" was never used before in the Kushite tradition. However, the only Egyptian ruler who had this title was none other than Psamtik II, who initially conquered Lower Nubia from Kush. This adoption of his enemy's title almost had the magical purpose of reverting history. The intention of conquest is also supported by his other royal titles, such as "Seizer of every land" or "Mighty Bull appearing-in Thebes."

Even though the Kushites obviously planned the conquest of Lower Nubia, and it indeed stopped being an Egyptian territory by the end of the 5th century, there is no evidence of Irike-Arnannote's involvement in the matter. Except for his titles, nothing confirms he led the Kushite army on a military expedition. The Egyptian rebellion ended in 404 BCE, and the kingship was returned to the royal family of Sais. The new pharaoh was Amyrtaios of Sais, and he moved Egypt's border north of the First Cataract, but the evidence of Kushite military garrisons in this area has yet to be found.

A document dated to the first and second year of Irike-Arnannote's rule mentions the internal trouble the Kingdom of Kush experienced. The nomadic Rehrehe tribes of Butana revolted and seized the territory north of Meroe, capturing all of the people and cattle that inhabited this area. The document describes the king's prayer for Amun's help and how he sent the Kushite army to deal with the rebellion while he stayed in the royal residency in Meroe. It is possible that, by tradition, Irike-Amannote had no right to lead the army, as his installment as the king of Kush was not yet over. As such, the kingdom was under the direct rule of Amun, and the army couldn't be led by anyone else but the god himself.

Tradition demanded that Irike-Arnannote be crowned in different locations around the kingdom, so the process of coronating a new king could take up to a few years. This didn't mean the future king couldn't assume his duties before the ceremonies were done. It simply meant the kingdom was directly ruled by the gods in the time period between the two kings. Irike-Arnannote was crowned in Meroe, Napata, Kawa, and Pnubs. During his ceremonial coronation tour, he had to deal with a rebellion of the Medjay nomadic people, who he defeated easily.

The fact that the new king had to deal with the nomadic tribes who occupied the territory between the Nile and the Red Sea speaks about the scale of the Kingdom of Kush during this period. However, the nomadic tribes and their way of living were difficult to integrate into the centralized government. Societies that were constantly on the move were hard to control, but Kush greatly depended on the cattle they provided and couldn't simply abandon them.

The socio-economic aspect of the Kingdom of Kush during the rule of Irike-Arnannote remains hidden, but it is obvious that the relationship with Egypt was diminished. This is shown not only in the lack of Egyptian items but also in the texts, which are all written in the corrupted Egyptian language, meaning the education of priests was no longer relying on the Egyptian tradition. It is unknown when exactly Kush moved away from the usage of the Egyptian language, but it is obvious that by the late 5th century, the Kushites developed their own language: Meroitic. But even though they spoke in their indigenous language, Egyptian was the official language for written documents. However, the Kushite priests didn't follow the contemporary trends of Egyptian writing, but they also moved further away from the tradition. Still, they failed to come up with their own style, and the result was grammatically incorrect Egyptian. Meroitic would become the official language of writing much later, at the dawn of the 3rd century.

The Kushite throne passed to Baskakeren, whose reign was very brief. He was succeeded by King Harsiyotef, who ruled approximately from 404 until 369 BCE. This king left a written document in the temple of Amun in Napata, in which he describes nine military victories he acquired during the first thirty-five years of his reign. Five out of these nine victories were against the nomadic tribes in the northern Butana region. Two listed military expeditions were led to Lower Nubia, while another two were against the nomadic peoples of Rehrehe and Medjay, who occupied central parts of the Kingdom of Kush. It is not clear whether the king led these expeditions personally, although it is known that Harsiyotef sent his servant to lead the Kushite troops in a Lower Nubian campaign in his eleventh regnal year. Because the rest of the campaigns lack this type of side note, it is safe to presume the other expeditions were led by Harsiyotef.

The expedition to Lower Nubia in his eleventh regnal year is of particular interest. The document describes how the rebels besieged the town of Mirgissa, after which the king sent a relief army. But the interesting fact is the position of this town. It lays beyond the First Cataract of the Nile, which suggests that by the time of Harsiyotef's rule, Kush was not only in control of Lower Nubia up to the Second Cataract, but it also controlled the territories to the north, between the First and Second Cataracts. The fact the rebels fled to Aswan after the Kushite army arrived means that Egypt was somehow involved in the conflict, but it is unknown to what extent.

In the eighteenth and twenty-third year of Harsiyotef's rule, a war was fought against the wealthy nomadic tribes. Their main occupation was cattle-breeding and trading. Because of their wealth, their constant moving, and social status, it was difficult for the king to assert his dominance on these tribes. Believing they had some political influence, these tribes would often rebel against the centralized government, which didn't suit their lifestyle. Since a centralized government meant that all of the power was concentrated in the big administrative cities, in order for one to prosper, he needed to stay near them. For people who constantly moved from one territory to another, depending on the season, a centralized government meant the loss of business opportunities.

But it wasn't only the lack of opportunities that bothered the nomads. They were wealthy because they owned great numbers of cattle that could be exported. Naturally, the king wanted his share of the cattle profit. If nothing else, he wanted the nomads to spend their wealth in the cities, where the taxes and tributes had to be paid directly to him. There are even indications of the kings of Kush trying to insert special higher taxes on the cattle-breeders based on their prestige.

The last Kushite king to be buried at the Nuri necropolis near Napata was Nastasen. He was probably the son of Harsiyotef, although he didn't inherit the throne directly from him. There may have been three kings who ruled before Nastasen, who were all probably his brothers. He probably ruled somewhere between 335 and 310 BCE, although the exact years are difficult to conclude. Since the lowest chambers of his tomb at Nuri were flooded by underground waters, it seems there is much to be discovered about this king. Because of the flooding, the tomb was sealed early, and it seems that grave robbers left it undisturbed. Archaeologists are working on it tirelessly, but many items were destroyed due to the constant exposure to water.

However, Nastasen left behind a stela with a long, historically important text, which gives us insight into his kingship and the Kushite government during the last decades of the 4th century. Nastasen's Stela is his enthronement document, and it emphasizes the king's dynastic ties with Harsiyotef. Because of this, many scholars assume direct descendancy took place, but there is a theory that claims that Nastasen would not have to emphasize his relationship with Harsiyotef if he was actually his son. Since there is no evidence to suggest otherwise, the belief in the father-son relationship remains.

Similar to Harsiyotef's stela, Nastasen's lists military conflicts that occurred during the first eight years of his rule. Many of them were ceremonial conflicts or the end of minor rebellions. However, the sheer number of them suggests that the territorial integrity acquired by Harsiyotef had to be defended, which could not have been an easy task. Lower Nubia was still administered by the local chiefs under the condition that they recognize the Kushite king as their superior. However, this didn't stop them from rebelling. In the south of the country, the continuous dissatisfaction of the nomadic tribes escalated to armed conflicts on a few occasions. Each time, Nastasen was victorious, and he detailed all the war booty he gathered. The amount of gold and cattle listed on his stela as war gains is astonishing, but considering that the Kushite nomadic tribes were among the richest people of the kingdom, it is not impossible.

The later years of Nastasen's rule were probably affected by the second conquest of Egypt by the Persian Empire (343–332 BCE), the Macedonian rule of Alexander the Great (332 BCE), and the later Ptolemaic Dynasty (beginning in 323 BCE). There is some evidence the Macedonians entered the territories of Kush as early as the reign of Ptolemy I. However, all these conflicts were concentrated around the Egyptian-Kushite border regions, indicating that it was the Kushites who were the aggressors. It is possible Nastasen saw an opportunity in the internal Egyptian struggle during the early years of Ptolemaic rule and that he led the attack with the intention of gaining the territories of Upper Egypt. However, there is no evidence of his success or his rule in the southern parts of Egypt.

A tale of the romantic relationship between Alexander the Great and Meroitic Queen Candance is nothing more than a product of the imagination of Pseudo-Callisthenes, the author of *Alexander Romance*. He wrote how Alexander attacked Kush in 332 BCE, but the queen prepared her army, and she rode in front of it on a huge war elephant. Seeing the might of Queen Candance, Alexander gave up conquering Kush, and he returned to Egypt. However, that wasn't the end of their contact. Through diplomatic connections, Alexander started a romantic affair with her. As a side note, the Greeks and Romans were wrong to assume that Candace was the name of this queen. In fact, this was the Latinized form of the Kushite title "Kandake," which would be used by the king's sister or a wife who was to bear the successor to the throne. The sister was only appointed with this title if the king had no wife capable of giving him a successor. She was chosen as a Queen Mother, and her son would be the successor to the throne. No matter how exotic and attractive the story of Alexander and Candance might sound, the only truth in it was the existence of diplomatic connections between the Kingdom of Kush and Alexander's Egypt.

Nastasen's successor moved the royal burial place from Nuri near Napata to Gebel Barkal. This move might have been caused by the dynastic change, but it is more probable the true motive was the lack of elevated space for the royal tombs. As we saw, Nastasen's tomb was flooded by underground waters because it was not elevated enough. His successors were probably aware of this problem, and because the afterlife plays such a huge part in the lives of pious rulers, the importance of proper burial grounds was enormous.

Aktisanes succeeded Nastasen and founded the new necropolis, where the pyramids, which were far less opulent, testify hard times followed in Kush. Observing the first tombs built at the Gebel Barkal site, it seems that the poverty of the kingdom lasted during the reigns of the next three or four kings. This poverty might have been caused by the failed military efforts of these kings in Upper Egypt. The constant war cost the kingdom, and not even the riches of the nomadic tribes helped.

The obvious poverty of the kingdom was further deepened by the Nubian campaign of Ptolemy II in 274 BCE. His motive for war with Kush wasn't the conquest of lands but rather securing the trade routes along the Nile. Ptolemy's expedition to Nubia wasn't against Kush, as he sought to establish safe trade with the kingdom. Instead, it was against the chiefs and tribes of Lower Nubia, who posed a serious threat to the trade caravans. Because of this, Ptolemy had the plan to annex this territory and renew the good relations between Egypt and Kush.

In the past, Egypt had lost its supply of war elephants because the Macedonian successor states in the region cut it off from the Indian subcontinent. An alternative source of elephants could be found in the southernmost regions of Kush, where these animals roamed freely. Even though Kushites used elephants, their knowledge in capturing and training them was very limited. Egyptian experts needed safe passage to the territories where they could hunt the animals and from which they could transport them back to Egypt with little effort. Ptolemy had two routes in mind: the land road along the Nile that led beyond the Fifth Cataract and a route that would take him along the coast of the Red Sea. To successfully use either of these trade routes, he needed to bypass Lower Nubia.

But the annexation of Lower Nubia also meant that the gold mines of the area would pass into Egyptian hands, and this was something the Kushites opposed. A conflict was imminent, and even though Kush lost, it also received tremendous benefits from it. The trade routes opened by the Egyptians brought prosperity to Kush, and the kingdom went through another cultural renaissance. Egypt didn't only renew its economic relationship with the Kingdom of Kush, but it also started importing its own intellectuals and craftsmen.

Chapter 6 – The Meroitic Dynasty

The Meroe Pyramids
https://en.wikipedia.org/wiki/Mero%C3%AB#/media/
File:NubianMeroePyramids30sep2005(2).jpg

Egypt's annexation of Lower Nubia and its trade contract with Kush brought new opportunities. Ptolemy's kingdom didn't limit its trade to the Kushite territory; it also went beyond to African states farther south and the Horn of Africa. But all the imported goods, such as exotic animals, timber, aromatic woods, and raw materials, had to pass through Kush, which means the kingdom had the right to collect the transport tax.

Because of this trade with the lands in the Horn of Africa, the southern regions of the Kingdom of Kush started developing at a great speed, especially the regions of Butana and Gezira. But the exponential growth of wealth through trade resulted in political changes, specifically dynastical change. The story of this change was preserved by a Greek scholar of the 2nd century: Agatharchides of Cnidus. His version of events is often quoted, but it is also misunderstood. Primarily, Agatharchides was a geographer, and historical accuracy did not concern him much. Through his writing, he tried to display the superiority of Greek culture over the traditional belief systems of other nations. This is why his story of Kushite politics needs to be taken with a grain of salt.

According to Agatharchides, the priests in Meroe had so much power that they ordered kings to die whenever they wanted to change the ruler. They pretended to receive a message directly from the gods, and the king could not refuse such an order. The Greek scholar continues to describe the people of Kush as simple-minded and ingrained in their tradition, unable to speak out against the all-powerful priests. But King Ergamenes, who had training in Greek philosophy, was of strong enough mind to ignore the priests' order to die. Instead, he raised an army and slaughtered all the priests of Meroe. Agatharchides also states his own opinion of Ergamenes, saying how he was worthy of being king because of his determination.

The story is obviously made up to demean the people of Kush and their traditions, as well as to make a point of the "supreme" Greek philosophy. The story's hero, Ergamenes, had Greek education, and the readers can see the obvious triumph of reason over superstition. But there is some truth in the story of Agatharchides. The kings of Kush needed legitimation from the oracles, and priests had enormous power in Meroe (though not enough to order kings to die). The story is also probably right about King Ergamenes raising an army, but in reality, he didn't slaughter the priests but won a dynastic struggle over the Kushite throne.

But who was King Ergamenes? Surely, this is a Greek name. In fact, it's the Hellenized version of his Kushite name, so history doesn't really know which king Agatharchides wrote about. The Hellenized name could be a derivative of either Arakamani (Arkamaniqo) or Arqamani. Because of this, scholars tend to believe that Agatharchides merged two kings into one semi-mythical Ergamenes.

King Arakamani is known for separating the state from the church by attacking the priests in the Amun temple of Napata. Because of this, some historians are eager to believe that he was the true Ergamenes of Agatharchides's story. But he did more than that. To separate the priests from the concept of power people associated them with, he moved the capital from Napata to Meroe. Although some scholars believe he didn't move the capital but only the necropolis, he is still considered to be the first king of the Meroitic period of Kush.

The fact that Arakamani took the title "The Heart of Re Rejoices," which belonged to Pharaoh Ahmose of the Twenty-Sixth Dynasty, suggests he used the army to defeat his opponent and climb the Kushite throne. Ahmose was the only Egyptian pharaoh who used this title, and he never hid the fact that he was a usurper. If Arakamani borrowed the title from the usurper pharaoh, it is quite possible he was trying to say that he came to power in a similar way. Kushite kings were known for borrowing titles from Egyptian rulers with whom they wanted to be associated, and it was more likely no different in the case of Arakamani.

His transfer of the royal necropolis to the city of Meroe might suggest the new dynasty had hereditary ties with the south of the kingdom. Even though we don't know when Arakamani exactly ruled (we cannot even begin to guess when he moved the capital to Meroe), it is known that it all occurred in the early 3rd century BCE, as this Kushite king was the contemporary of Ptolemy II Philopator, who ruled Egypt from 285 until 246 BCE.

The Meroitic period of the Kingdom of Kush is believed to have started with the reign of Arakamani. Even though the power was now concentrated in the southern capital of Meroe, the whole kingdom underwent developments, which have been attributed to this king and his successor, Amanislo. The theory that just the burial grounds of the royal family were moved from Napata to Meroe is supported by the fact that Amanislo started renovation works on the royal residency in Napata.

The Kingdom of Kush and Ptolemaic Egypt

The Kingdom of Kush continued its trade relations with Egypt even though it tried to gain the territories of Lower Nubia after Egypt's conquest by Alexander the Great. The Ptolemaic Dynasty of Egypt, which was a result of that conquest, continued the good trade relations between the two kingdoms, and it also renewed the connection between Kushite and Egyptian priests. This connection brought a new cultural renaissance to the Kingdom of Kush.

After the death of Alexander the Great, his close generals fought for power over the lands he conquered. The result was splitting the territories, and Egypt was taken by Ptolemy, who proclaimed himself a pharaoh. Ptolemy was Macedonian, and with his rule, the Hellenic influence began not just in Egypt but in all the territories in close proximity. The Kingdom of Kush already shared the religion and culture of Egypt, and when Hellenism came, it could not resist its influence. The architecture and the official art of monument building were probably influenced by Hellenism the most, but religious concepts and iconography followed. Even the minor arts, such as pottery painting, succumbed to the Hellenistic style.

Egypt didn't remain untouched by Kush. Luxury items from all over Africa were transported to Egypt via the route that led through the Kingdom of Kush, so the economic importance of this kingdom continued to grow. In fact, the lands of Kush were always a tempting source of gold until, finally, Ptolemy II launched an attack, during which he gained access to the gold mines of Wadi Allaqi and Gabgaba, south of Aswan. The rule of the Ptolemaic Dynasty also brought Hellenistic scholars, who showed interest in Kushite culture, religion, and people. However, the kings of Kush also developed contact with Upper Egypt, where the rebels who opposed the Ptolemaic rule thrived. It seemed that Kush was constantly trying to undermine the Egyptian rule, perhaps because they wanted to retrieve the old glory of the Twenty-Fifth Dynasty or just to retrieve their old territories of Lower Nubia, which they succeeded in doing so in 207 BCE.

The leader of Upper Egypt's revolt against Ptolemy IV was of Nubian descent, Hor-Wennofer (Horwennefer), who captured Thebes in 205 BCE. There, he was accepted as a pharaoh, and he ruled for six years. His son, Ankh-Wennofer (Ankhwennefer), succeeded him, and he ruled for nineteen years before he was deposed by Ptolemy V Epiphanes in 186 BCE. Even though it seems the Kushites supported the revolt of Upper Egypt, they only did it because they saw an opportunity to expand their territories over Lower Nubia between the First and Second Cataracts. However, there is no evidence to confirm that Kush managed to gain territories beyond the First Cataract. To further support the theory that the Kingdom of Kush had something to do with the Upper Egypt revolt is the agreement between the two kingdoms, which resulted in Meroitic forces fighting on the side of Ankh-Wennofer against Ptolemy V. The Ptolemaic Dynasty did not only regain the throne of Egypt, but it also managed to take back the territories of Lower Nubia by 172 BCE.

Kush was ruled by Arqamani and Adikhalamani during the period of Egyptian revolts. Because they are represented in the temples of Lower Nubia, as that part was returned under the Kushite rule, the early Egyptologists thought of them as under-kings in the Nubian regions who ruled under the pharaoh. It was later, during the excavations in the Kingdom of Kush, that historians learned they were both great kings of separate kingdoms and contemporaries of Ptolemy IV.

It is a general opinion that trade along the Nile Valley was interrupted during the rebellion and the return of the Ptolemaic Dynasty to the throne of Egypt. Although the elephant trade was revived shortly after the revolt in Egypt, it again died by the middle of the 2nd century, probably because India started supplying the Ptolemaic Dynasty with their superior breed of war elephants.

By 150 BCE, Lower Nubia was a separate administrative unit led by the rulers of Thebes. This type of administration in this disputed territory continued through the reign of the Ptolemaic Dynasty and Roman rule of Egypt. The non-Egyptian citizens of Lower Nubia were ruled by their own indigenous chiefs, who also acted as Egyptian officials. This means that the integration of native politics into the Egyptian administration occurred in Lower Nubia.

The decades that followed the rule of Adikhalamani in the Kingdom of Kush remain obscure, as there is not enough evidence to offer an image of the events that followed. However, it was during this time, somewhere during the late 2nd and early 1st centuries, that Egypt retreated from the southern parts of Lower Nubia. There is evidence from 117 to 115 BCE of Elephantine priests complaining about low incomes. By the time of Ptolemy XII's rule (80–58, 55–51), there is no mention of him or his successors south of Philae (near the First Cataract).

Kingdom of Kush between the 3rd and 1st Centuries

The Kingdom of Kush was completely integrated into international trade with the Hellenistic world during the 3rd century. As a result, luxury items produced in Kush, such as pottery and exotic animals, were found all over the known world. But even though there is a lack of evidence that Kush imported items from abroad (except from Egypt), they were influenced by the Greeks, mostly on an intellectual and cultural level. They started implementing the Hellenistic style in their own arts, and they started developing the Hellenistic belief system, which was applied to the Egyptian pantheon.

Trade opened the Kingdom of Kush to the outside world, and with the wealth and power they accumulated, the expansion of the kingdom began. This time, it was a diplomatic expansion through the development of new alliances, especially with its southern neighbors. As a result of the overall development of the kingdom, the redistribution of the people occurred. The rich elite started inhabiting provinces at the edges of the kingdom because international trade led them farther away from the main cities. While domestic trade still happened in the big trade hubs such as Napata and Meroe, international trade was concentrated in the fringe provinces, where trade caravans crossed from one kingdom to another.

The development of diplomatic relations with the south led people to reside in the southern provinces. New port cities were raised along the Red Sea, which meant people started concentrating in the east too. But the movement of people doesn't mean the cities were empty. They were still very much alive, for they were still the administrative centers of the kingdom, where all the power and riches were gathered in the hands of the royal family and the priesthood.

In the cities, the temple-building projects of kings continued, but this time, the changes in style were obvious. The Kingdom of Kush followed the latest trends of Ptolemaic Egypt, so the new buildings obviously followed the Hellenistic structure. Old temples were abandoned during the mid-3rd century in favor of the newly built ones. Such a fate occurred to the temple of Amun in Napata, which had been built by the Twenty-Fifth Dynasty. Even though it was still standing during the 3rd and most of the 2nd century, no rituals were performed there, and there is no archaeological or written evidence that speaks about this temple from that point on.

During the reign of King Arnekhamani, the royal residence was moved to Musawwarat es-Sufra. Aside from the royal palace complex, the site includes at least one temple. The royal residency complex, which extended over 64,000 square meters, is one of the most important achievements of the Kushite culture. It is obvious that Egyptian artists were involved in the building of the temple in Musawwarat es-Sufra, as it follows the contemporary style of Ptolemaic Egypt. The cult of Arensnuphis, to whom the temple was dedicated, emerged as the first known deity that belonged only to the Kushites. The mythological role of this deity is unknown, but eventually, it spread throughout the regions of Nubia that were controlled by Egypt.

Scholars speculate the new deity was needed to legitimize the new dynasty. The new royal family had roots in the Butana region, where the aspect of a warrior king was even more important than in the rest of the kingdom. Arensnuphis, who is depicted as a lion and human, was the warrior-hunter god of the desert. But these characteristics were now attributed to all the gods who were associated with the ideology of kingship: Amun, Apedemak, and Sebiumeker.

Another interesting change to the kingship ideology is seen in the depiction of the royal costume, which was found in the new temple and royal residency in Musawwarat es-Sufra. Based on the contemporary Ptolemaic fashion, the kings of Kush started wearing three-part royal costumes: a tunic, a shoulder-fastened wrap-over, and a sash that was tied around the right shoulder and the chest. All of this was already in use from the period of the Twenty-Fifth Dynasty; however, the style changed. The wrap-over used to be a belt, which was ceremonially tied by the god Amun in recognition of the rule of the new king. Now the belt was a tasseled cord, which was tied over the shoulder in the same manner as the belt used to be, but this time, it was associated with the Kushite warrior-hunter god Arensnuphis.

The economic and intellectual contacts with the Hellenized Egypt of the Ptolemaic Dynasty brought changes to the Kushite society as well. New communities started rising in both the southern and northern regions of the kingdom, and the development of Meroitic hieroglyphic and cursive scripture occurred. The cursive writing is of particular interest, as it was developed to serve the purposes of the growing elite. Literacy was also no longer reserved for the kings and the priests. It allowed communication aside from administrative purposes, and it was used by the provincial elite, local administrators, lower ranks of the priesthood, wives, and children of middle-class merchants and members of the non-royal elites. The cursive scripture became a staple of the elite society, and it was used in all spheres of their life.

The first known ruling queen on the throne of Kush was Queen Shanakhdakheto. Her name was the first to be written in Meroitic hieroglyphic scripture, and it was wrongly believed to belong to a king. Her rule took place around the beginning of the 2nd century, according to the style of her pyramid and the items found in; however, the exact years of her rule are unknown. Her ancestors are unknown, and there is no evidence that would tell us which king she succeeded. However, her depiction in the mortuary chamber, as well as in Temple F at Naqa, clearly shows she was a ruler. Her title was "Son of Re, Lord of the Two Lands," and she was adorned with jewels to show off her power and richness.

In this depiction, she is accompanied by a prince, probably her royal consort, who is displayed wearing a Greek-style tunic and a simple diadem, clearly stating his non-ruling position. The men standing next to Queen Shanakhdakheto are shown touching her crown, which can be translated as the transfer of power to her. This might mean that a female ruler needed to prove her connections to the dynasty and the right to rule. It cannot be an accident that the next ruling queen, Amanirenas (one hundred years after Shanakhdakheto), had the same depiction in her reliefs.

Shanakhdakheto's rule offers much to the understanding of Kushite culture. Not only was she the first female ruler, but the relief of her mortuary chamber shows just how much the Kingdom of Kush departed from the Egyptian tradition during the new Meroitic Dynasty. For example, the funerary rite of the "neck dancers" is depicted in her tomb, portraying Kushite customs instead of Egypt's, which had been popular up until the 3rd century. The "neck dancers" relief shows a procession of musicians and dancers who accompanied the queen on her last journey to the afterlife. Another purely Kushite custom is depicted in a relief where men hold arrows during the funerary procession. The fact that Queen Shanakhdakheto had a one-part title, "Son of Re, Lord of the Two Lands," instead of a five-part title like the Egyptian custom dictated, shows that the Meroitic Dynasty truly distanced itself from their predecessors and Egypt.

The changes that were so obvious in the depiction of Queen Shanakhdakheto become even more emphasized during the rule of her successor, King Tanydamani (approximately 180–140 BCE). During their reigns, human and animal sacrifices in the elite burial sites occurred. Whether these were connected somehow with the change in the Kushite religion or were remnants of the indigenous traditions remains unknown. At first, during the beginning of the 2nd century, the sacrifices, mostly horses and humans, were found in the tombs of the rich elite. But during the late 2nd and early 1st centuries BCE, they started appearing in the royal tombs as well. This speaks in favor of new religious practices instead of the reemergence of indigenous traditions.

The first monument written in Meroitic cursive scripture is the stela of King Tanydamani. Unfortunately, this scripture has yet to be completely deciphered. Besides some theonyms (references to deities), nothing else is understood. However, these theonyms indicate that the kingship dogma was unchanged and that the cults of Amun of Napata and Amun of Thebes were still alive in the Kingdom of Kush.

The Kingdom of Kush and Rome

The 1st century was filled with events concerning Egypt. The kingdom became the Roman province and was under the direct rule of the Senate in the year 80 BCE, although it had been influenced by Rome for much longer. For instance, events and figures, such as Julius Caesar, Mark Antony, the suicide of Cleopatra and the murder of her son, the kingship of Octavian, and the first Roman prefect of Egypt, Cornelius Gallus, all affected the Kingdom of Kush.

Egypt wasn't thrilled with the Roman rule, and a rebellion in Upper Egypt occurred in 29 BCE. Meroitic Kush was involved in it. Cornelius Gaius managed to quickly crush the rebellion, but to ensure it wouldn't happen again, he led his forces on a campaign in Lower Nubia. The records of his campaign are recorded on a stela in Philae in three different languages: Latin, Greek, and Egyptian. According to the stela, Egypt's prefect was victorious in two battles against the rebels, and he conquered five cities, after which he continued to the Nubian region.

The reason for the rebellion was the high taxes in Upper Egypt, according to the Greek historian Strabo. But how did Meroe fit in the rebellion? It seems the Kushite rulers at the time wanted to establish a new border with Egypt beyond the First Cataract. They supported the rebellion in order to weaken the kingdom and easily take over the territories they wanted. This theory is supported by the list of cities Cornelius Gaius conquered: Boresis, Koptos, Keramike, Diospolis Magna, and Ophelion, which were all near Thebes.

Cornelius Gaius managed to retake all of Lower Nubia and make a special administrative unit out of it, just as it was during the early Ptolemaic period. He did this in order to block any further Meroitic advances in the region and to cut them off from their allies in Upper Egypt. A *tyrannos* was installed to oversee the region, although it is unknown how much power this title brought. The *tyrannos* of Lower Nubia was probably a title given to a local chief who would assert control over both Egyptian and non-Egyptian citizens.

The Greek version of Gaius's victory stela indicates that the region conquered from the Meroitic Dynasty became a vassal chiefdom, which means that the Roman plan for the whole Kingdom of Kush was to turn it into a vassal state. It is possible Emperor Augustus even planned the annexation of the whole kingdom; however, this never came to be, due to the strong opposition of the Kushites.

In the summer of 25 BCE, Emperor Augustus ordered the second prefect of Egypt to lead a campaign against Arabia Felix. He installed Gaius Petronius in this position, who was to lead the campaign against the Kingdom of Kush at the same time. However, Gaius Petronius was completely unprepared when Meroitic Queen Kandake Amanirenas decided to launch the first strike. The Kushites crossed the First Cataract and attacked Philae, Aswan, and Elephantine. Egypt was provoked, and Petronius had to quickly organize a counterattack. By the winter of 24 BCE, Emperor Augustus received the first Meroitic prisoners, who were sent by the prefect of Egypt. Strabo records that when Petronius asked the Meroitic forces why they attacked, they replied they were angered by the tax collectors. But this account of the conflict seems to indicate that the Meroitic forces were just a part of another rebellion in Lower Nubia, not a part of the direct attack sent by Queen Kandake.

At the time of the events, Queen Amanirenas was known as Queen Kandake, who was associated with King Teriteqas. It was only after his death that she succeeded him and became the second ruling queen of the Kingdom of Kush. During the conflict with Rome, she resided in Napata, where Petronius decided to launch the next attack. According to Strabo, Amanirenas offered peace to Petronius, but he disregarded it and attacked the city. Napata quickly fell and was razed to the ground. However, Petronius was unable to establish Roman rule over the conquered Kushite territories, and he had to turn back to Egypt. Despite this, a new border was established at Qasr Ibrim, where the Roman garrison guarded the restored Nubian administrative unit.

Emperor Augustus soon changed the Roman imperial policy of annexing the vassal states, so the campaign in the Kingdom of Kush was abandoned. Instead, Meroe was treated as a client state, and the ambassador of Kush was sent to negotiate peace with Augustus. The loss of Napata was irrelevant to the Kingdom of Kush, as their true center of power was now in Meroe. Meroe's opposition to Rome continued even after Napata was lost, and after only two years, Queen Amanirenas launched another attack. She led the forces to Qasr Ibrim, where the Roman garrison had just exhausted its supplies. But Petronius heard of her plans in time, and he arrived at the site before the Meroitic army. This forced the Kushite queen to negotiate peace. Taxes were imposed on the kingdom, and the borders were moved even farther south to Hiera Sycaminos, modern-day Maharraqa.

The territory between the First and Second Cataracts now belonged to the Roman Empire and was annexed. But the people who lived there were Aethiopians, and Rome was smart enough to leave the administration of the region in the hands of the domestic elite. The whole region was observed as a military zone, with its civil administration only loosely attached to Roman Egypt. The area between the First and Second Cataracts acted as a buffer zone, which was supposed to stop any Kushite attempt of expanding to the north.

Queen Amanirenas's successor wasn't her son, Akinidad, who appears next to her in all the depictions. She was instead succeeded by another ruling queen, but the reasons for this remain unknown. The inscriptions found in the Amun temple of Meroe, as well as in Temple T at Kawa, indicate that she was another wife of King Teriteqas and that she inherited the throne after Amanirenas because Akinidad wasn't accepted as the legitimate heir. We know he was alive because he is depicted next to Queen Amanishakheto, the new ruler, just as he was next to her predecessor.

The fourth female ruler followed right after, and she was known as Queen Nawidemak. She ruled around the 1ˢᵗ century CE. Nothing is known about this queen, but scholars suggest there was some kind of dynastic trouble since there three concessive female rulers. However, there is no evidence to support this theory, except that the place of royal burials was often changed during this period.

The Kingdom of Kush recovered from the Roman attack by the middle of the 1ˢᵗ century CE, and the Meroitic Dynasty led the kingdom into a new era of prosperity, which was displayed through excessive monument and temple building, intellectual achievements, and art. The two kings most deserving of recognition when it comes to the building projects were Natakamani and his co-regent Amanitore. They dedicated their rule to construction works and restoring monuments. To list just a few of their projects: the Amun sanctuary at Gebel Barkal, Amun Temple at Naqa, Isis Temple at both Waq and Naqa, a royal palace at Gebel Barkal, and the later Amun temple at Meroe City. The art style of this period suggests a renewed Egyptian influence, but this time, Roman details were prevalent instead of Ptolemaic ones. Even the throne names of the rulers were once more written in Egyptian hieroglyphs, but the Kushite title "Son of Re" remained unchanged.

Chapter 7 – The Last Centuries of the Kingdom of Kush

In the period between the late 1st and 3rd centuries, there was an explosion in the development of new settlements. However, this did not necessarily mean an increase of citizens in Kush; rather, it was a shift toward the new trade routes and agricultural regions. Caravan settlements, as well as small agricultural communities, started developing into urban settlements, much like towns or even cities. This period is rich in archaeological findings, which help cast light on the social structure of the kingdom and less on the royal and political history. The first impression when observing this period of Kushite history is peace and prosperity, but this might be false, as the kings were still valued for their warrior abilities, which would suggest some kind of conflict occurred.

The distribution of the monuments throughout the kingdom indicates the government was still centralized, which was a tradition brought down to Kush from the Egyptian Twenty-Fifth Dynasty. However, unlike the patrilineal succession of Egypt, the succession in the Kingdom of Kush continued to follow its own collateral line. Even female rulers were attested, and their kingship was seen as legitimate in the Kushite kingship ideology.

The troubles the kings had with controlling the nomadic tribes who inhabited their lands were finally solved in the 3rd century CE. The kings could finally follow the movement of the nomads and implement a taxation system on the *hafirs*, the water stations these tribes stopped at with their cattle. In Butana alone, there were around 800 *hafirs* registered. They had artificial water sources and were built as round enclosures; they were around 70 to 250 meters (230 to 820 feet) wide and 7 meters (23 feet) high. Through the season, the nomads would gather around these water sources, which always had a temple attached to them. They exemplified the royal power over the people, as they served the purpose of assimilating the non-sedentary peoples into the culture of Meroitic Kush. One of the biggest *hafirs* was the reservoir at Musawwarat es-Sufra, and it could fill a volume of up to 135,000 cubic meters (around 35,663,227 gallons).

In the regions of Lower Nubia that were still under Roman control, the non-Egyptian and non-Roman elite continued to rule in an administrative capacity over the mostly Aethiopian citizens. One powerful family would emerge from the elite that would allow the Meroitic Dynasty to take part in local affairs from the 2nd to 4th century CE. In fact, around the middle of the 3rd century, the Kushites regained full authority over the region. The powerful elite family who made this possible is known as the Wayekiye family, after the name of one of its most prominent members. This family continued to be mentioned in Meroitic royal texts for the next eight generations.

The members of the Wayekiye family held high offices in the administration and priesthood. Wayekiye himself belonged to the fourth generation of the family and had the title of "Chief Wizard of the King of Kush." He was also the hont-priest of Sothis and the waab-priest of the "five living stars." Both titles represent a certain level of purity that brought about certain responsibilities. The last title is generally accepted to mean that Wayekiye was an astronomer, while the previous two titles are similar to the ancient Greek title of a prophet. If Wayekiye's titles correspond to the similar titles found in Egypt, this would mean that he was the royal astronomer and astrologist, which further implies he had excessive education as the "writer of the sacred books." His duties were to measure the time, the length of the days during the course of the year, and to define the length of night and day over the change of the seasons.

His title of "Chief Wizard of the King of Kush" is of special interest, as it implies strong connections with the royal Meroitic Dynasty and with Lower Nubia, in which Wayekiye resided. The most obvious conclusion would be that Wayekiye received this royal title in return for bringing the Roman-Egyptian time measurement system to the Meroitic court. Wayekiye lived in Roman Lower Nubia but was invited to the Kingdom of Kush, where he and his wife were eventually buried. This proves that Wayekiye was the connection between the two kingdoms, as he brought Egyptian knowledge to the Kushites. This alone leads scholars to think that Wayekiye was also an instrument of political influence.

The other two prominent members of the Wayekiye family were Manitawawi and Hornakhtyotef II, and they belonged to the fourth and fifth generation, respectively. They were important because their titles indicate they were no longer in the service of the Roman province of Egypt, as they were proclaimed to be the "princes of Triacontaschoenus" (the Roman term for Lower Nubia) and "agents of the King of the Land of Nubia." This means they were governors of Lower Nubia who were appointed by the king of Meroe, indicating that Lower Nubia was again in the hands of the Kingdom of Kush.

The Meroitic supremacy in Lower Nubia is confirmed by the lack of Roman garrisons stationed there. The Roman withdrawal from the region may have been influenced by the plague, which occurred in around 200 CE, and the border was moved to the north, to Aswan. Meroitic Kush took Lower Nubia without conflict, but the area was constantly raided by the nomadic Troglodytes and Blemmyae. The Kushites had to set up immediate defenses throughout the eastern desert and the hills of the Red Sea coast.

To the south of the Kingdom of Kush, a new kingdom rose to power and threatened the borders. This was the Kingdom of Aksum, and it is probable that because of their advances, the Meroitic kings were forced to expand their territories to the north. An unknown king of Aksum, who lived at the end of the 3rd century, led a military campaign against the northern tribes and even reached the city of Meroe. However, he was more interested in establishing a land route to Egypt for trading purposes. Aksum rose to such power that, during the end of the 3rd century, it took over the export of African goods to the Mediterranean world, becoming an economic rival of the Kingdom of Kush.

The Disappearance of the Kingdom of Kush

During the late 3rd and the beginning of the 4th century CE, the Kingdom of Kush was an administratively and socially well-developed state. The contemporary written evidence offers us a glimpse into the period when Lower Nubia was under the rule of a royal deputy. The Nile Valley was densely inhabited with towns and villages developing at an exponential rate. These areas were under the supervision of district officials, who were closely tied to the temple cults. The area of the Kush empire between the Second and Third Cataracts was under the administrative rule of a local chief, who held the title *sleqen*. He resided in Sedeinga, where rich pyramids were erected for the needs of the officials. Unfortunately, there is not much evidence that would introduce us to the governmental structure south of the Third Cataract. However, the number of settlements and their distribution suggests that the government of this area might have been very similar to the one in Lower Nubia.

By the middle of the 3rd century, Rome was in crisis. Their economy and government were on the decline in Egypt, and this influenced the Kingdom of Kush greatly. While the Roman government of Egypt would be reorganized under the rule of Diocletian (284–305 CE), the Kingdom of Kush would never be able to get back on its feet. To the south, the Kingdom of Aksum rose and seriously threatened the physical and economic integrity of Meroitic Kush.

Archaeological evidence suggests the Kingdom of Kush continued to thrive during the 3rd century, and it wasn't, just yet, concerned with the events outside its borders. It was at the end of the century that the outside influence began to negatively affect Kush. The disproportional development of the country is obvious at this time, with the south deteriorating while the north was rich enough to thrive for some time.

There is not much evidence to attest to what exactly happened in the Kingdom of Kush that made it disintegrate. The first problem seems to have appeared in the south. The large-scale migration of people occurred when the area was threatened by the Kingdom of Aksum. But it is only a theory that Aksum was involved since it was the most powerful neighbor of Kush. There is evidence that suggests that after the Kushites left, the southern parts of the kingdom were not inhabited with the Aksumites but by the Nobatae people of the desert, whose origins remain a mystery.

The king who ruled Kush during the late 3rd and the early 4th century was Yesebokheamani. It is possible that he was the king who asserted Meroitic control over Lower Nubia once the Romans withdrew. There is evidence of his visit to the Philae temple compound, as there are Meroitic inscriptions there commemorating this visit. A lion monument in Qasr Ibrim is also dedicated to Yesebokheamani, at least according to the Meroitic cursive scripture.

Roman Emperor Diocletian peacefully withdrew his forces from Lower Nubia, probably because of the threat posed by the Blemmyae tribes who lived between the Nile in Lower Nubia and the Red Sea. These tribes were aggressive toward Egypt, and they even started an alliance with the Meroitic Kushites. Instead of fighting them, Diocletian decided to let go of the territory and concentrated his power elsewhere. Sometime between the 3rd and 5th century CE, the Blemmyae organized themselves in larger units of tribal kingdoms. They concentrated their power and presented a threat to Upper Egypt and Lower Nubia. In order to keep their territories safe, the Meroitic kings allied themselves with the Blemmyae against Rome, and to keep them from threatening the Kingdom of Kush, they promised the tribes settlements in Lower Nubia, which belonged to Rome.

The last decades of the Kingdom of Kush and the Meroitic Dynasty are poorly recorded. The mortuary chapels of the last rulers offer evidence that the kingship ideology survived, as well as the collateral succession, which was traditional for Kush. The burial pyramids of the last five kings speak of the sudden economic decline of the kingdom. Although these pyramids contained much less in terms of objects, their architectural, artistic, and iconographic expression confirms the cultural continuity.

Although not much changed in the burial places of the kings and elite, a drastic change is noticeable in the houses of the common people who lived in the large cities of the south, including Meroe. The architecture in the south started changing and separating from the kind seen in the north of the kingdom. The large, spacious houses were replaced by smaller ones with mudbrick walls and tight rooms. However, these rooms were all positioned around a big courtyard. These types of houses were probably built for extended family members. The difference is so obvious that it speaks of the occurrence of a new type of habitation that was previously unknown in Meroe. The logical conclusion is that it was brought by immigrants who started inhabiting the city

At the end of Meroe's existence, evidence shows the temples were abandoned, even though people still occupied the city. The royal palace was also abandoned, and it instead served as a burial ground for the commoners, who placed their dead in the cuttings in the walls. At this time, during the 4th century, there was a lack of Kushite pottery, which means that the local production of luxury goods had already stopped and was replaced by the more archaic style ceramic wares. This new ceramic pottery was found in burial sites that didn't belong to the Meroitic people and is considered to belong to the period that immediately followed the disintegration of the Kingdom of Kush

The last Meroitic burial sites of the royals and elite members of society are dated to the middle of the 4th century. However, new burial styles for the common people, as well as the appearance of new but archaic art styles of common items, suggest the existence of two cultures in the transition period between Meroitic and Post-Meroitic. These two cultures had nothing in common, and the transition was not gradual at all. This means the new culture must have belonged to the newly arrived population who brought their tradition to Meroe.

In Hobagi, around sixty-five kilometers (forty miles) southwest of Meroe, early tombs of these rich immigrants were found. The tombs display all the signs of a tribal community, which had divided its semi-nomadic people into two social groups: warriors and cattle-breeders. These Post-Meroitic burial grounds belonged to the Noba people of the West Nile regions. However, the Hobagi site needs more excavations and detailed analysis of the findings in order to bring unbiased conclusions.

The Nobatae people occupied the regions west of the Nile, which expanded from the city of Meroe to the north, where the Bayuda region lay. The Nobatae people were ethnically the same as the occupants of the Nubian Nile Valley during the period of the New Kingdom (16th–11th century BCE). The conflicts between the Nobatae people and the Kingdom of Kush occurred as early as the 1st century CE, and the first settlement of these tribes in the Kushite territory was recorded in the 4th century by Aksumite King Ezana. He left behind textual evidence, which mentions a conflict between the Kingdom of Aksum and Meroe. In this document, the Nobatae were mentioned as the people who took the territories of northern Butana and Bayuda from the Meroitic kings.

Scholars believe the resettlement of the Nobatae people occurred on the invitation of the Kushite kings. Because of the growing threat that was the Kingdom of Aksum, it is possible that the Meroitic kings adopted the Roman strategy of *foederati*, binding the nomadic tribes in the service of the Kushite army with special treaties. But this is just a theory based on the lack of conflicts between the Nobatae and the Kushites in the early years of the resettlement. A similar system to the Roman *foederati* in Africa happened in the Kingdom of Aksum.

Their kings employed the vassal tribes in order to fight Meroe in the 4th century.

On two separate occasions, Meroe was occupied by the Aksumite kings, which is confirmed by the excavation of two Aksumite Triumphal Stelae, which were written in the Greek language. But historians cannot agree whether this meant the Kingdom of Kush became an Aksumite vassal or not. Nevertheless, the fact that the kings of Aksum resided in Meroe speaks about the weakness of Kush at the time. Aksum may not have been the destructor of the Kingdom of Kush, but it definitely contributed to it.

The end of the Meroitic Dynasty happened due to an expedition to Kush by Aksumite King Ezana (320–360 CE). He left the Triumphal Stelae in Meroe, but it remains unknown if he conquered the city or came to assist the Kushites against the rebelling Nobatae people. Whatever the case was, the Kingdom of Kush was already so weak that only a few years after Ezana's presence in Meroe, the Meroitic Dynasty disappeared.

The last royal burial place at Meroe belonged to Queen Amanipilade. The tomb itself is of very poor quality, but it still follows the traditional style of the Meroitic Dynasty. However, the kingdom didn't disappear with this queen. It continued to exist for several more decades, taking up the territories from Butana in the south to Lower Nubia in the north. But scholars call this political unit the Post-Meroitic successor state, and it was governed by the non-royal surviving deputies of an unknown ruler who resided in the south.

Around 420 CE, the deputies of Lower Nubia assumed royal titles and started the Ballana Dynasty and the Kingdom of Nobatia, by which the region of Nubia got its name. The Kingdom of Kush was no more. In its stead, new kingdoms rose: Nobatia, Makuria, and Alodia. They would soon convert to Christianity, and the old Egyptian and Kushite gods, such as Amun, Mut, Isis, and Arensnuphis, would be forgotten.

Chapter 8 – The Society of Kush

The excavations performed at Napata, Kawa, Musawwarat es-Sufra, and later Meroe didn't just allow us to learn about the chronology of the Kingdom of Kush, its rulers, and religion. The cities contained tools, art, and everyday items belonging to the common people. Based on these, we can reconstruct the basics of their lives, allowing us to understand the complexity of the Kushite society.

Through the ambivalent connection with Egypt, with whom the Kingdom of Kush was in constant conflict, we can observe the influences the two kingdoms had on each other when it came to cultural traditions, language, and scripture. Unfortunately, more excavations need to be done in the areas of the once-powerful Kingdom of Kush for us to understand all the nuances of the social structure of the kingdom. Little is known about the commoners, as they left no trails behind them. Based on what we know of Egypt and its influence on the Kushite culture, we can still hazard a guess, especially when it comes to the Twenty-Fifth Dynasty and their descendants, the Napatan Dynasty.

The Settlements of the Napatan Period

The first documents from the Napatan period show the territorial governmental structure and its implementation in the settlements that sprouted around the Amun temples and the royal residence. These settlements, including Kawa, Napata, and Meroe, consisted of Amun temples and the royal palace, which were made out of stone and brick. The settlements also contained workshops and habitation areas that catered to various layers of society. The workshops were not only for the local production of one settlement. In fact, they were huge spaces that supplied the whole kingdom with various items, such as pottery, ceramic wares, and later even iron tools. These workshops were under royal or temple authority, as they were not owned by individuals but by the kingdom. Some settlements had minor royal residencies instead of palaces, and they also had special open places dedicated to various temple festivals.

Life in the Middle Nile Region greatly depended on the river levels and the occasional changes in its course. The main agricultural hubs were concentrated there, as it was the most fertile region of the kingdom. However, none of the agricultural settlements shows any signs of consistency. The unpredictable flow of the Nile, as well as the political and religious trends of the period, often dictated the constant movement of people. Also, the quality of production might have dropped in some regions as the people moved in search of more fertile grounds. Unfortunately, there are not many excavations done on the agricultural settlements to reach any concrete conclusions of the people's movement and the density of the inhabited areas. As such, no conclusions can be drawn about the size of the agricultural settlements or their prosperity.

However, the kingdom's overall prosperity fluctuated, and it greatly depended on international trade and relations with Egypt. In previous chapters, we explained that even though there was a certain amount of conflict between Egypt and the Kingdom of Kush, the need for the trans-African trade routes often prevailed. Thus, the two kingdoms enjoyed various trade treaties that brought luxury African items to the Mediterranean world. But it was the control of these trade routes that often sparked conflict in the first place. It seems that Egypt and Kush were trapped in a circle of dependency and conflict.

Unlike agricultural settlements, the principal cities and towns showed signs of consistency. Scholars believe this was due to the careful selection of their geographical location, which benefited not just their economic status but also tactical defense. But the quality of life in these permanent settlements greatly depended on the political life of the kingdom. When the trade agreements with the neighboring kingdoms were in place, the quality of life in the city was high. But during times of conflict, it was greatly reduced by the lack of international income. But life in the city was also influenced by the wealth of the royal family and the elite of society, which was tightly connected to the kingdom's political background.

In Napata, there wasn't much change to the urban structure of the city. The only noticeable change was the relocation of the royal necropolis from the opposite bank of the river to the slopes of Gebel Barkal. The need for moving the necropolis might have come from the importance of Gebel Barkal in the religious rites of the Kushites. No changes in the structure of the Napatan habitation quarters were noticed.

In Meroe, the habitation quarters were divided from the royal palace and the temple of Amun by the various canals of the Nile. This was probably not done as a separation between the social classes but out of the need for irrigation, as the Nile gradually withdrew from the vicinity of the city. It was this change in the Nile Basin that probably led to the abandonment of the Amun temple in Meroe and the need for a new one.

Besides the agricultural settlements and the permanent capital cities, the Kingdom of Kush was also rich in trade caravans and military bases. These were seen as settlements, even though they were short-lived and often changed their location based on the need of traders or the defense of the kingdom. Most of the settlements discovered between the Third and First Cataracts of the Nile were of this type, and they belonged to the period of Ptolemaic rule in Egypt. Musawwarat es-Sufra is seen as a special type of settlement, known as the Great Enclosure, as this was a temple complex and a place of pilgrimage.

The Art

The Kingdom of Kush adopted its iconography from Egypt but only its style. For example, in Egypt, the representation of various peoples occurred, and iconography was available even to the commoners. This didn't happen in Kush. During the early Napatan period, human figure representation was reserved only for the images of gods and the members of the royal family. However, there were exceptions to the rule. Besides the nameless priests, an occurring feature in the Kushite reliefs, there are also carvings of some very important non-royal figures, such as heroes or administrative officials of great importance. Nonetheless, the representations of important figures never had a cult significance attached to it.

Aside from the relief carvings of the temples, royal palaces, and tombs, figure representations of nameless people occur in the minor arts, such as pottery. But here, the human figure has a purely ornamental purpose and was not attached to a specific individual. In the cases where the human figure was not used as an ornament, it was used as a personification of the concept of kingship. This means that humans were represented only as the king's attendants or his mourners after his death.

Monumental sculptures were always reserved for the divine and the royal. The purpose of the colossal Kushite monuments was to show the connection between the god and the king. Here, Kush always managed to follow contemporary Egyptian trends. The early period of Kush represented the gods with eternally youthful faces and slender figures, while the kings were represented more realistically, with facial features with ethnic characteristics. However, the Kushites never depicted the actual person, as they were more generalized to the Nubian ethnicity. Unlike the divine, the royal bodies were muscular, influenced by the Old and Middle Kingdom art of Egypt.

The best representation of Kushite ethnic realism is probably the statue of Queen Amanimalolo from the Amun temple of Napata. She is represented as a heavy, steatopygous person, but this was not how she actually looked. This was the idol of beauty among the Kushite royal females, and it was also a sign of fertility. Because the succession in Kush was matrilineal, the fertility of the king's wife or mother was the sign of legitimating the kingship.

The monumental depictions of kings changed after the reign of King Aspelta, as they were under the direct influence of the Twenty-Sixth Dynasty. No longer were the kings represented as muscular figures but rather as smooth-limbed yet not thin men. The king now lacked muscles, but the thickness of his body was a representation of his power. At first, archaeologists thought the lack of details in sculptures meant a decline in its quality, but it turns out it was just an artistic trend that quickly passed. During the late Napatan and early Meroitic periods, the traditional depiction of muscles surfaced again.

Art existed in Kush only as a form of expression of religious dogmas and kingship ideologies. While the ornamentation of luxury items was common, it didn't really represent the art of the Kushite culture, as it mostly followed the contemporary Egyptian style. Mass production of everyday clay and iron items were intended for both internal use and for exportation. However, the luxury items found in the royal tombs of the temples suggest the existence of small royal workshops, where the luxury items would have been made by artists. Unfortunately, many of the Kushite tombs were plundered on more than one occasion, and there are only a handful of such items. Because of this, it is practically impossible to determine if they were, indeed, of Kushite origin in the first place.

Government and the Social Structure of the Meroitic Period

During the early Meroitic period, the first signs of the social division between the north and the south of the kingdom appear. In the north, between the First and Third Cataracts, the professional elite arose, while in the south, there is no evidence yet of any kind of elite. This might be due to the lack of archaeological excavations in the region, but it is more probable that the society of the south had different traditional values. After all, the north was in constant contact with Egypt and was influenced by it, especially through the rivalry in Lower Nubia. But the difference in social structure doesn't mean the administration of the kingdom greatly varied in different regions. In fact, the official titles were the same in the north as in the south.

As for the economy of the kingdom during the Meroitic period, it was interconnected with the administration, whether it was civic, royal, or temple administration. Governmental officials collected taxes, but at the same time, they were also temple officials who collected donations. This is because the Amun temples and the royal residency were seen as two bodies of the same spirit; the king was a ruler on Earth, but at the same time, he was divine. Later, we will explain the connection between religion and kingship in more detail, as they were inseparable in Kush until the very end, while in Egypt, the separation of Amun and the king occurred during the Ptolemaic period.

The creation of the Meroitic cursive script during the 2nd century BCE might have been due to the need for a new administrative direction of the kingdom. Nonetheless, the new script was primarily used by the growing professional class of the Kingdom of Kush.

Lower Nubia was under the control of Meroitic officials, who held the title *peseto*. He had a role similar to a modern-day viceroy, and he was appointed from a non-royal elite family. The title was not hereditary, although there were cases where it remained in the extended family. During the 3rd century BCE, new titles started appearing in Lower Nubia, and they show the tight connection between Meroitic Kush and Roman Egypt. The titles were *apote Arome-li-se* ("envoy to Rome") and *apote-lh Arome-li-se* ("great envoy to Rome"), and they were reserved for the administrative or priestly elite of Lower Nubia.

During the late 1st century BCE, one more title emerged in the Kingdom of Kush. This time, it was bound to the area between the Second and Third Cataracts. Priests were appointed to the position of *sleqen*, which was a similar administrative title to the *peseto* of Lower Nubia.

Due to the lack of evidence, nothing is known about the lower classes of the Kushite society. However, excavating the various settlements can give us some insight into the number of people who inhabited certain regions. It is safe to say that Meroe, as a royal, religious, and trade center, attracted people of all classes. On the other hand, Naqa, which lay to the south, lacks any non-luxury habitats, and it is presumed this settlement was inhabited only by the provincial elite. The nomadic cattle-breeders cannot be tracked through history. Because of their way of life and constant movements, they left no trails, and it is impossible to prescribe any archaeological findings to them. It is a different case with the agricultural societies of Lower Nubia, though. There, villages consisting of approximately twenty to thirty houses were excavated. The graves found in the vicinity of these villages attest that the life for a farmer was of a high standard. The items excavated both in the villages and in the cemeteries confirm this. However, the small size of these settlements suggests the farmers were not considered to be a low class of society but, in fact, middle to elite.

South of Maharraqa, a number of cemeteries were found, which are believed to have belonged to the warrior class. The items found with the buried bodies are very poor, but the burials are arranged in close groups, which indicates some kind of military organization. Unfortunately, these cemeteries cannot give any evidence of Kushite military life. The textual evidence always focuses on the king as the ultimate warrior and never speaks of a regular army. Even the small number of weapons found during the excavations of the Kushite sites were always connected to the kings and were found only in their burial places. Unless more excavations are done, and more sites are found, the defenses of the Kushite kingdom and its army will remain completely unknown.

The succession in the Kingdom of Kush was matrilineal, and this wasn't only a rule for the kings and queens. The archaeological evidence found in the tombs of the elite confirms that a similar matrilineal line of succession was followed. The name of the mother is always listed first in the tombs of the deceased, whether they were high priests, clerks, or viceroys of Lower Nubia. The mother legitimized the social status of the individual, but it is not clear if the elite society just imitated royal decorum or if it was the generally accepted rule of succession that simply transcended all social layers.

Social status in Kushite culture was very important, even for the afterlife. This is displayed not only in the richness of the tombs of the elite but also through the hierarchy of the elite gravesites. A *peseto* was always buried in the tallest and richest pyramid, which was positioned in the center of the graveyard, and he was surrounded not just by his family but also by his subordinates. Priests were buried at a distance from the *pesetos* and their families to show the unique importance of their class.

Kushite Religion and Kingship

The religion of the Kingdom of Kush was polytheistic, and it was greatly influenced by Egypt. During the first excavations in the region, which were performed in the early 20th century, a mistake was made that identified the Kushite culture as Egyptian. The first archaeologists didn't make the difference between the two kingdoms, as Lower Nubia was believed to be a constant part of Egypt. However, excessive research proved that Nubia was a specific region, although it was influenced by Egypt to the point where the border between the two cultures becomes nearly invisible. Kush was never inhabited by many Egyptians, as it had its own indigenous people. But parts of it were under Egyptian rule, which was enough for the excessive Egyptianization of the local populace.

This Egyptianization continued once the kings of Kush conquered Egypt and ruled it as the Twenty-Fifth Dynasty. Although the Kingdom of Kush started showing some signs of its own independent culture during the late Napatan period, it was the Meroitic Dynasty that distanced itself from Egypt's influence. However, the constant contact, whether it was through war or through trade agreements, proved that the ties with Egypt were never really cut.

The Kingdom of Kush emerged as a successor state to the Egyptian rule over the Nubian regions. As such, it adopted the Egyptian belief system. Already existing Egyptian temples were the foundation for the development of the Kushite religion. At the capital of Napata, the Great Temple of Amun was erected during the 13th century BCE, probably during the reign of Thutmose III and Ramesses II. This temple, just as the god it was dedicated to, Amun, played a central role in the religious lives of the Kushites. Since the reign of King Piye, this was where all the kings had to be crowned before they embarked on their coronation tour. Even when the capital of the kingdom was moved to Meroe, the kings of the Meroitic Dynasty came to Napata to be crowned at its Amun temple.

The god Amun was of Egyptian origin, but his importance was brought to new dimensions in the Kingdom of Kush. Amun, pronounced as Amane or Amani in the language of Kush, was of national importance. He was the father of the kings and ruled above all. Amun was first attested during the Old Kingdom, where he was a god of the wind. But later, he merged with other deities and eventually was elevated to the position of the main deity in the Egyptian religion. When Amun was merged with the god Re to form Amun-Re, he became the solar deity, father of all gods and men, and the creator of the universe. In Kush, Amun was represented with the head of a ram. This was actually remnants of the old Kerma culture and their solar deity, which was represented as a ram. When the Egyptians first conquered the Kerma society, they identified their main deity with Amun.

The connection between Amun and the Kushite kings starts as early as the rule of King Kashta. Although he is not known for having the royal title similar to those of later kings, Kashta's respect for Amun is shown by the promotion of his daughter to the position of the Divine Adoratrice of Amun. This was the first known event in which a king of Kush used the power of a deity to promote himself and his dynasty. The connection between Amun and the Kushite kings began. From this point on, the kings were seen as the sons of

Amun, and as such, they had their own cults. Amun's priests and oracles were able to hear the messages of the god, and they were the ones who would announce the next king. Once the new king was crowned at the Napatan temple of Amun at Gebel Barkal, he would start a journey through his land to be crowned in each major temple dedicated to this god. Depending on the vastness of territories a king ruled, this ceremony could take up to a few years. During this period, the kingdom was under the direct rule of Amun. Even though the new king could assume all of his duties, he was not considered a true king until he finished the coronation tour.

Other details of the Kushite religion are sparse, largely due to the fact that the Meroitic language is still not completely deciphered. Not much is known about the other Kushite gods, and all we can do is interpret the reliefs of them in the temples and tombs of the kings and queens. It seems that other Egyptian gods were worshiped in Kush, such as the moon god Khonsu, Thoth, Re, Khnum, and the goddesses Hathor, Isis, and Mut.

But it seems that the gods were not worshiped in all the regions of the kingdom. The god of the Nile Cataracts, Khonsu, was especially important in the Nile alley. Lower Nubia also worshiped Horus, while the south of the kingdom saw little mention of him. Mortuary tradition was also adopted from Egypt, and with it came the worship of the Egyptian mortuary deities, such as Osiris, his sister Isis, Anubis, and Nephthys. Isis became the wife of Amun in a later period and was no longer associated with the mortuary rites. Instead, she became the mythological mother of the Kushite kings.

As explained in previous chapters, with the rise of the Meroitic Dynasty, a greater separation from Egypt's influence occurred. The Meroitic period saw the introduction of several deities that were clearly not of Egyptian origin. However, it is impossible to claim that they were purely Kushite gods. The influence of their southern neighbors is possible but not yet confirmed. These deities were Apedemak, a warrior god associated with kingship; his wife, Amesemi, the goddess of protection; Sekhmet, the mother of Apedemak and the goddess of anger and chaos; and Bastet, the goddess of motherhood. All these Meroitic deities are connected to the south of the kingdom, while the north continued to mainly worship Egyptian gods.

Animals also played an important role in the Kushite religion, and they are often depicted in temple reliefs. Cattle were associated with the north, where it played an important part in various religious processions. In the south, the most sacred animal was the elephant. Other animals connected with religion were baboons and crocodiles. The details of religious rituals remain obscure, but from the reliefs at the temples and tombs, we can conclude that offerings of food and drink played an important role. Later on, animal and human sacrifices were introduced, but they disappeared quickly.

Just like in Egypt, the afterlife was a very important religious aspect for the Kushites. They believed that life continued after death, and this was why they were buried with various items they might need in the afterlife, from jewelry and pottery to food offerings and even their favorite pets. The Egyptian feature of the mortuary rites adopted by the Meroitic kingdom was the erection of the *Ba* statues. These were statues of birds with human heads representing the deceased. *Ba* was the part of the soul that could travel between the worlds, while *Ka* was the part of the soul that was the life force and needed a new body. This new body was another statue, made in the likeness of the deceased so the life force could recognize its owner. There was even a third part of the soul that, after death, traveled to unite with the gods.

Conclusion

Although it is often overlooked and greatly misunderstood, the Kingdom of Kush was, without a doubt, a major power in the ancient world. It was the southern frontier of the classical world, and with its deserts, gold mines, and exotic animals and items, it intrigued the rulers of Egypt as much as the ancient Greeks and Romans. The kingdom, settled in the Middle Nile Valley, went through three distinct phases. Although it was not yet the Kingdom of Kush, the Kerma culture united the peoples of the Nubian region once it was abandoned by Egypt. The first rulers who dreamed about a single civilization didn't just manage to start their own kingdom but also managed to conquer powerful Egypt.

King Kashta was named by the Egyptians, and his name simply means "The Kushite." This means that the growing power of his united kingdom was already strong enough to be recognized. It became an attribute worthy of being the name of a king. Although greatly influenced by Egypt, Kush was always a separate political entity, whose leaders defended its riches. Although the northern part, Lower Nubia, often saw the change of the administration as well as the ruler, its people remained Kushites by culture, ethnicity, and nature.

During the Meroitic Dynasty, Lower Nubia was lost, but its priesthood and people continued to gravitate toward the south. The region was torn by various conflicts (Egypt, Assyria, Meroe, and Rome), but it was also inhabited by rebellious people with their own idea of independence. Later, they founded their own Kingdom of Nobatia, which gave the modern name "Nubia" to the whole region.

The Meroitic Kingdom of Kush thrived under the new dynasty, but the center of power moved from the northern capital of Napata to the southern city of Meroe. This was the period when Kush started standing on its own. Although it may have been influenced by the migrating nomadic tribes, it started developing its own southern culture, first through language, new gods, and scripture.

But nothing lasts forever. The world was changing around the Kingdom of Kush, and it couldn't retain its borders. Scholars believe the rise of the southern Kingdom of Aksum brought about the destruction of Kush in one way or another. While some believe it was a direct conquest that brought Kush to its end, others believe such destruction never even occurred. According to them, Kush vanished peacefully, dissipating into the more powerful neighboring kingdoms who took over its role in the economy and the political scene of the African continent.

Here's another book by Captivating History
that you might be interested in

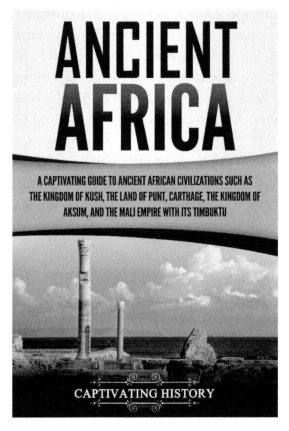

References

Bonnet, C., & Louis, H. (2019). *The Black Kingdom of the Nile*. Harvard University Press.

Dixon, D. M. (1964). The Origin of the Kingdom of Kush (Napata-Meroe). *The Journal of Egyptian Archaeology, 50*, 121. https://doi.org/10.2307/3855745

Kendall, T. (1997). *Kerma and the Kingdom of Kush, 2500-1500 B.C.: The Archaeological Discovery of an Ancient Nubian Empire*. National Museum of African Art, Smithsonian Institution.

László Török. (1995). *The Birth of an Ancient African Kingdom: Kush and Her Myth of the State in the First Millennium BC*. Université Charles-De-Gaulle.

Trigger, B. G., & Welsby, D. A. (2000). The Kingdom of Kush: The Napatan and Meroitic Empires. *The International Journal of African Historical Studies, 33*(1), 212. https://doi.org/10.2307/220314

Williams, B. (2001). Kerma and the Kingdom of Kush 2500-1500 B.C.: The Archaeological Discovery of an Ancient Nubian Empire. Timothy Kendall. *Journal of Near Eastern Studies, 60*(3), 1-197. https://doi.org/10.1086/468921

Made in the USA
Las Vegas, NV
23 August 2021